Fancyboy

Fancyboy Walker Brown

Founded in Provincetown

FIRST EDITION

Printed in the United States of America

LIBRARY OF CONGRESS RECORD

Name: Brown, Walker, 1968 — author.
Title: TITLE / AUTHOR
Edition: First edition.
Published: Atlanta : Unbound Edition Press, 2026.

LCCN: 2025930711
LCCN Permalink: https://lccn.loc.gov/2025930711
ISBN: 979-8-9919575-2-6 (fine softcover)

Designed by Eleanor Safe and Joseph Floresca
Printed by Bookmobile, Minneapolis, MN
Distributed by Itasca Books

123456789

Unbound Edition Press
Founded in Provincetown

This book is lovingly dedicated to Karen Smith-Firebaugh, who first taught me to be proud of myself.

May every child know the gift of such a beautiful soul.

Contents

Fancyboy

Preface: From Maui, With Love

With all of the beauty on the island, my family's properties are my favorite places on Maui. Over time, each of my immediate family members has eventually found themselves here. In the early 2000s, my youngest brother Jesse moved here, and soon after so did my brother Jay with his girlfriend, Karmen. My parents eventually did the same. They all found properties on the North Shore, in a beautiful town called Haiku. Each property is bluff side, at the end of a hairpin road shaded with overgrown vines and plantain banana leaves. Each piece of land is covered with indigenous plants, with countless palms and fruiting trees. I love nothing more than to find fruits from the yard and turn them into our dinner and concoctions for tiki drinks. There are varieties of banana, lilikoi, guava, citrus, and papaya. Fairy-like orchids and bromeliads hang from the trees.

They seem magical, these bits of the natural world. The views down tropical gulches with rushing waterfalls burst alive with blooming melon-colored African tulip trees. Several large rainbow eucalyptus trees with multicolored, aspen-like bark tower above. Color is everywhere – pinkish red, bright violet, creamy white, pale fuchsia, and deep crimson – with each one stirring up various emotions or inspiring me in some way. The smell of flowers perfumes the air, as an orchestra of tropical bird calls echoes from a hidden place. My mother tends to her plentiful garden, where she has pots full of fresh herbs.

I am lucky to be spending several months here working on this book, recalling memories of family, kitchens, restaurants, and the profound role food has played in uncovering, shaping, and affirming my authentic life.

Each time I leave Maui to head home to Atlanta, it gets harder. Though Atlanta can be a great city, it does not have the magic or color that Maui has. There is no salty air, no lightness in the breeze, no spirit that encompasses everything on the island – plants, animals, people, the water, the sand, the wind. Island lore puts it this way: *if you are there, you belong there*. My family definitely does. Maybe I will fully belong to this island one day, too. A part of me is always here.

My family has always had an adventuresome essence. My parents brought us up during the counterculture era of the 1960s and they have never lost that sense of exploration. Thankfully, they passed this attitude and passion on to their children, including me.

Fancyboy is my love letter to them, to the wonder they instilled in me, and to the space they always created for me to be me, starting in the most unlikely of places.

From Commune to Paradise

The first kitchen I truly loved was one without walls. We called it "the kitchen shelter," a makeshift structure my family built on a commune in Canada when I was four years old. While other kids played in the dirt, I spent hours arranging wildflowers in Mason jars and setting our rough-hewn table with whatever beauty I could find — pine cones, colored leaves, interesting stones. I didn't know then that these small acts of decoration were early signs of who I would become.

The kitchen shelter was the heart of our creativity — a 10-foot-high, 25-foot-wide tunnel of sheet plastic and small trees that I transformed into my first canvas for beauty. The foundation was dirt, the walls barely existed, built from saplings cut at their base and arched from side to side in a row to create a gentle rainbow-shaped tunnel. Sheet plastic draped over these arches formed a 50-foot-long shelter that glowed with filtered sunlight. At the end stood my favorite thing on the commune: a refurbished enamel wood-burning kitchen stove, complete with an oven, bread warming compartments, and a flattop for heating pots and pans. It became my fixation, my destination, the thing I miss most about that place.

Along the sides of the shelter, shelves burst with Mason jars of all things picked, pickled, and preserved. I loved arranging and rearranging these jars by color, creating patterns that caught the dappled light. Large coolers filled with fresh ice held our perishables, and a 10-gallon Coleman water cooler with a spout stood ready to dispense well water for drinking and cooking. In this simple space, I found endless possibilities for creating beauty.

The kitchen shelter's design came from *The Whole Earth Catalog*, a bible of sorts for commune dwellers of the era. But while others saw it as purely functional, I saw it as a space for transformation. The shelter wasn't just a place to cook and store food — it was where our community came together, where music filled the air alongside the aromas of cooking, where I first learned that making something beautiful could bring joy to others.

My parents were young when they had me — my mom gave birth right after high school graduation, and my dad was only a year older. It was the late 1960s, and my brother Jay was born a year after me, the same week Neil Armstrong took "one small step for man, and one giant leap for mankind." By the time I was four, they were swept up in the counterculture movement that would shape my early years.

The late 1960s and early 1970s crackled with revolution. The Vietnam War raged, the Black Panthers had fully formed, and Watergate dominated headlines. Young people were taking to the streets, fighting for civil rights, advocating for women's equality alongside Gloria Steinem, and reimagining how life could be lived. Minds were being expanded, sometimes with the help of marijuana and LSD, and new forms of music — psychedelic rock, folk, soul — provided the soundtrack to this cultural transformation. It was an electric time to be a four-year-old amidst it all. How lucky I was. How lucky I am.

The younger generation had grown weary of the post-World War II "plastic fantastic" consumer mentality and Nixon conservatism. They weren't just seeking political change — they were crafting new ways of living. Communes sprouted up across North America, with people choosing to live "off the grid," raising families in handcrafted dwellings without electricity. These weren't rough shanties, but beautiful structures of wood and stone, with geometric rooms, skylights, and repurposed church windows. My childhood home would become one of these spaces where creativity flourished in unexpected ways.

My parents took me out of kindergarten in Perrysburg, Ohio to begin this adventure. They were young and seeking something different from the status quo, though they didn't fully know what waited ahead. We had our red Carry-All Chevy truck, which resembled a small bus with a roomy back interior that my parents had transformed into a tiny mobile home, complete with a sleeping area and portable outdoor kitchen. We set out for a small village in Quebec, where a community of American and French-Canadian youth welcomed us. After living in a tent for a few months, we found our home with this commune and its magical kitchen in the woods.

Big community meals were made in combined effort, filling the kitchen shelter with warmth and purpose. The smell of wild rice cooking in sesame oil still takes me back there. Even now, I can smell barley, garbanzo beans, and Indian-spiced lentils stewing for hours, their aromas creating an invisible dome of comfort around our gathering space. These usually vegetarian dishes were shared among all the commune dwellers, young and old alike. But my favorite was something simpler — my dad's garlic spaghetti, which he'd whip up during a craving. Just pasta tossed with fresh garlic, salt, and pepper. I still make that aromatic spaghetti to this day, each bite a thread connecting me to those earliest memories of food as both sustenance and love.

The kitchen shelter was more than just a place to cook. It was our community center, where musicians — including my dad — would gather to play fiddles, mandolins, and banjos. A jig or two would be danced to an old Appalachian bluegrass piece, or a sing-along folk tune would break out, like a collective smile. I learned early that beauty could be found everywhere — in the steam rising from a pot, in the way light caught the Mason jars, in the rhythm of chopping vegetables, in the harmony of voices raised in song.

My parents didn't have much money then, but they were young, proud, and brave. I have no memory of feeling poor — it was a proud poor, one of choice for my parents and their friends. The "plastic fantastic" world, as they called it, with all its conveniences, was something they willingly sacrificed for a chance to do things differently and better. For me and my brothers, it was a constant adventure: we didn't have to ask to go camping since we already were. While other kids my age were watching TV dinners spin in newfangled microwaves, I was watching my father coax magic from simple ingredients on our wood-burning stove.

It was on that stove that my father would make his garlic spaghetti, a dish that taught me how a few basic ingredients, treated with care and attention, could create something extraordinary. The pasta would steam in the cool evening air, the garlic would sizzle and turn golden, and the whole shelter would fill with an aroma that drew people from across the commune. I'd watch him carefully, noting how he waited for just the right moment to add each ingredient, how he knew exactly when the garlic was perfectly golden, how he tossed the pasta with such confidence and joy.

My friends who grew up more conventionally likely don't know the sound of a fiddle on a mountain night, or the feeling of reading by a kerosene lantern's flicker. Have they run by a cold creek into a fern valley below? Have they been stained from lovingly picked berries? I hope so. If not, I hope they can taste these experiences in the food I make for them. It's all in there, in every dish.

Years later, when I began cooking professionally, I would return to these early lessons: the importance of simplicity, the power of fresh ingredients, the way food can bring people together. But most importantly, I learned that cooking isn't just about feeding people — it's about creating moments of beauty, even magic, out of the most basic elements. This is perhaps best exemplified in my father's garlic spaghetti, a dish that remains both a comfort and an inspiration.

Dad's Aromatic Garlic Spaghetti

This might be the first dish I can truly remember — not just its taste, but its entire sensory experience. The way the garlic's aroma would fill our kitchen shelter, how the steam would rise in the cool Canadian evening, how my father's hands would move with such certainty as he stirred. It's possibly the simplest recipe in this book, but it taught me my first and most important lesson about cooking: that beauty often lies in simplicity, in doing a few things perfectly rather than many things adequately.

When I make it now, in my modern kitchen so different from that commune shelter, the scent of garlic hitting hot oil still takes me back to those early days. It reminds me that fancy ingredients aren't necessary for creating something spectacular—it's the care and attention you bring to even the most basic elements that matters.

Ingredients:

1 pound regular spaghetti noodles
4 cloves of garlic, peeled, sliced and minced
Olive oil
Salt and pepper

Directions:

In a large stock pot or Dutch oven, bring 3 quarts of water, 1 teaspoon olive oil, and 2 teaspoons salt to a boil. Watch for the moment when the surface of the water begins to dance.

Follow the directions on the box for al dente-style cooked spaghetti. Add the spaghetti to the boiling water and cook, stirring frequently for approximately 10 minutes until done. The pasta should be tender but still have a slight bite.

Reserve ½ cup hot pasta water before straining and set aside.

Strain the water from the pasta in a colander, discarding the remaining water.

Add ¼ cup of oil and the reserved pasta water back to the pot.

Add the garlic and return the pot to medium — high heat, bringing it to a simmer.

Cook the garlic in the simmering water and oil for about 2 minutes. Listen for the moment when the sizzle becomes musical and gentle. Do not burn the garlic. Turn the heat down if needed.

Add the spaghetti to the garlic, oil and water mixture and toss with tongs until well coated. The pasta should glisten, and the garlic should be evenly distributed.

Remove from the heat and add salt and pepper to taste, tossing again with the tongs.

Serve immediately, while the steam still carries the aroma of garlic through the air.

Notes:

There's a reason this dish has stayed with me for decades. On the surface, it's just pasta with garlic and oil — but like so many simple things, its beauty lies in the details. The key is to cook the garlic just until it turns golden and fragrant, before it browns and becomes bitter. When I teach this recipe to others, I tell them to listen for the moment when the garlic's sizzle in the oil becomes gentle and musical — that's when you know it's ready.

While the garlic spaghetti taught me about simplicity, it was my father's molasses cookies that first showed me how food could be magic. In our commune kitchen, where everything was meant to be practical and purposeful, these cookies were pure pleasure — a small act of rebellion against utility, a celebration of sweetness for its own sake. The aroma of ginger and allspice would transform our humble kitchen shelter into something extraordinary, drawing people from across the commune like a spell.

I remember watching my father make them, his hands dusted with flour, the spices lined up like jewels. In a world where we'd rejected so many conventional comforts, these cookies were our luxury. The warmth of the wood stove, the golden glow of molasses being poured, the way the dough would slowly transform from sticky chaos into perfect circles — it was all a kind of alchemy that fascinated me. While other kids my age might have been eating store-bought cookies from plastic packages, I was learning that the most precious things often come from our own hands.

Even now, decades later, my father still makes these cookies for me sometimes. When he does, that first warm, spicy bite brings back everything: the filtered sunlight through our plastic walls, the sound of folk music drifting in from outside, the feeling that even in the simplest surroundings, there was room for something special, something fancy.

Dad's Molasses Cookies

(Makes about 3 dozen 2-inch cookies)

Crispy and light, these cookies carry the warmth of those commune days in every bite. While perfect any time of year, their warming spices make them especially welcome during the holiday season. The aroma alone is worth the effort, filling your kitchen with the same magic that once filled our simple shelter. Looking back now, it seems like a whole other planet, but these cookies bring it all rushing back.

Ingredients:

1 stick (8 tablespoons) unsalted butter

½ cup granulated sugar

1 egg, beaten

¾ cup molasses

2½ cups all-purpose flour

1 tsp. baking soda

¼ tsp. kosher salt

¼ tsp. allspice

¼ tsp. ground clove

¼ tsp. ground nutmeg

1 tsp. powdered ginger

1 tsp. ground cinnamon

⅛ tsp. cayenne pepper (optional)

½ cup buttermilk

1 tsp. good sea salt for dusting (optional)

Directions:

Preheat the oven to 350 degrees and place the rack in the middle position. The warmth will soon fill your kitchen with memories.

Set the buttermilk aside to come to room temperature.

In a small bowl, beat the egg with a fork until well blended — it should be sunny and bright.

In a medium bowl, use a mixer to beat the butter and sugar until soft and creamed, or use the wire whip of a stand mixer. The mixture should be pale and fluffy, like the clouds that would drift over our shelter.

Add the beaten egg to the mixture and mix on medium until well blended.

Add the molasses and mix again until well blended. Watch how it ripples and swirls, dark and mysterious.

In a large mixing bowl, combine the dry ingredients with a wire whisk until well blended: the flour, baking soda, spices, and kosher salt (save the sea salt for later.)

Add approximately half of the butter and sugar mixture to the dry mixed ingredients and stir with a wooden spoon until blended. Then alternately add half the buttermilk and stir, then again the other half of the butter and sugar mixture, then again the remaining buttermilk. Stir until well incorporated.

Form rounded teaspoons from the dough and drop onto an ungreased cookie sheet, leaving 2 inches between each round.

Bake at 350 degrees for 7-10 minutes or until lightly browned. Be careful not to overcook as not to toughen.

Loosen with a spatula and place on a cooling rack.

Sprinkle the cookies lightly with the sea salt while they are still hot by pinching a little and spreading lightly from at least 6 inches above.

I cook today to visit yesterday or dream of tomorrow. This is what food does — it arches across time and place, bringing us together around a warm stove. Every time I bake these molasses cookies, I'm both that wide-eyed child in the kitchen shelter and the chef I would become. The simple act of mixing spices into molasses connects me to my father's hands doing the same decades ago, to all the moments of warmth and acceptance in that unconventional childhood.

Living on the commune wasn't about deprivation — it was about choosing a different kind of richness. My parents chose to do things differently, to show their children that beauty could be found in unexpected places, to create feasts from whatever the land and season provided.

The kitchen shelter taught me my first lessons about beauty — that it doesn't require fancy ingredients or expensive tools, just attention and care. These lessons would shape my entire life, though I didn't know it then. While other children were playing with plastic toys that would soon be forgotten, I was learning to create moments of delight from the simplest materials: wild flowers in Mason jars, perfectly arranged serving dishes, cookies that filled the air with spice and warmth.

Our time in Canada would eventually end, as all seasons do. The South was calling — Tennessee, with its own kinds of beauty waiting to be discovered. But I carried the kitchen shelter with me in my heart, its lessons about simplicity and creativity becoming part of who I am. Every time I dress a table or plate a dish, every time I transform simple ingredients into something special, I'm that child again, learning that beauty can be found anywhere if you know how to look for it.

Today, my cooking brings together all these threads — the counterculture simplicity of the commune, the warmth of family gatherings, the joy of creating beauty from basic elements. Whether I'm making my father's garlic spaghetti in my Atlanta kitchen or baking his molasses cookies for friends, I'm connecting past and present, simple and fancy, the child I was and the chef I became.

When I visit Maui now, where my family has found another kind of paradise, I see echoes of those commune days. The same appreciation for natural beauty, the same joy in simple pleasures, the same understanding that the most precious things often come from our own hands. The kitchen shelter may be long gone, but its spirit lives on in every meal I create, every table I set, every moment of beauty I bring into being.

Back to the Garden

One of my most vivid memories is picking fresh Silver Queen corn on a balmy summer evening, the symphony of katydids filling the woodland Tennessee air. The corn was extra crisp and sweet, and we always started the water heating on the stove before anything else. My mom taught me that timing was everything — the less time between picking and cooking, the sweeter the corn would be, the more its natural beauty would shine through. This was my first lesson in the garden: that nature offers its own kind of perfection, if you know when to look for it.

After our time on the Canadian commune, we had packed the Carry-All and headed south for warmer weather. My dad's sister sold us about 15 acres of their land in the beautiful woods outside a town called Sewanee, on the lush plateau of Monteagle Mountain in Tennessee's Cumberland Gap. We lived in an area called Jump-Off Road — a name that captured both the thrill and the risk of starting over.

At first, we lived in a tent on a hand-built platform next to a kitchen shelter just like the one we'd built in Quebec. During the summer months, my dad worked on building a one-room home that would be more suitable for the coming winter, especially since my mother was pregnant with my youngest brother, Jesse, who was due in December. This dwelling would be lovingly called the "electric shack" — our first concession to modern convenience, with a power line brought onto the land.

The electric shack was small but perfectly suited to our needs — a kitchenette, a built-in bed for my parents, and enough space beneath it for me and my brother Jay to sleep on a foam mattress. What adults saw as cramped quarters, we transformed into our own magical realm.

That space under the bed became our private universe, a permanent blanket fort where we would perform puppet shows, create art projects, and play board games. Our creativity flourished in that confined space, perhaps because of its limitations rather than despite them.

There was a crib for our newborn brother and a small potbelly stove to keep us all warm. That first winter, as we waited for dad to complete our bigger home down by the creek, we lived in a kind of enchanted miniature world. I remember the Christmas when Jesse was newly born — somehow Santa Claus managed to sneak an electric toy train into our one-room home, setting it up around the tree while we slept. Even in that tiny space, there was room for magic.

When we finally moved into the bigger home down the hill, we discovered a different kind of magic in the large vegetable garden we planted each spring. Unlike the commune's shared gardens, this was our own piece of earth to tend. There were at least four long rows of Silver Queen corn and a row of tomatoes of several varieties — my favorites were the cherry and little yellow pear tomatoes, which looked to me like tiny jewels in the sunlight.

The garden became my first canvas for creating beauty outdoors. We had rows of bell peppers, carrots, yellow hook-neck squash, zucchini, sweet onions, radishes, okra, snow peas, snap beans, asparagus, potatoes, lettuces, melons, and gourds. But it wasn't just vegetables — there were herbs and edible flowers called nasturtiums and marigolds, along with ornamental zinnias, towering sunflowers and delphinium. Even then, I understood that a garden needed both the practical and the purely beautiful.

We would make nearly all our meals with these gorgeous vegetables, letting nature guide our menu. Each day began with taking baskets into the garden, gathering whatever looked ripest.

The daily fresh basket of homegrown veggies would inspire what we'd make for dinner that night. Years later, when I worked in Atlanta's finest restaurants, I would return to this principle — letting what's in season and at its peak determine the dish. We would also preserve much of the produce through canning and pickling for fall and winter, like so many pre-boomer generations before us.

My mom would transform our harvest into feasts: squash casseroles, sweet onion and cucumber salads, and plates of sliced tomatoes still warm from the sun and sprinkled with salt. I remember baked peppers stuffed with rice and herbs, roasted sweet potatoes slathered with butter, and stir fries of broccoli, carrots, and snow peas. And always salads with a variety of vegetables served over fresh Bibb lettuce with nasturtium petals atop — my first lessons in plating, though I didn't know it then.

But the garden wasn't just about the vegetables we planted. The woods around us offered their own kind of produce section. In this area of Tennessee, blueberries were abundant throughout the forests, and blackberries grew in huge patches along gravel roads leading to our property. Picking berries with my mother and brothers was more than just gathering food — it was an education in patience, in searching for beauty in hidden places. She would turn these wild treasures into extraordinary pies with flaky, homemade crusts, all oozing with aromatic juices.

I can still picture her cutting the leftover pie dough scraps into rustic geometric shapes, baking them into cookies with a dusting of cinnamon and sugar — a little something to hold us over while the pies cooled. Even then, I was learning that nothing beautiful should go to waste, that every scrap could be transformed into something special.

Things were really changing during that time. Vegetable gardens had become quite popular in the counterculture movement, just like in Quebec. Growing and putting up our own vegetables was something we were proud of and essential to the way we lived — off the grid. This was an important, slow beginning of how we look at shopping, cooking, and eating today. The counterculture's experimental lifestyle helped usher in the health-food movement of the 1970s and early 1980s. It was the precursor to the organic movement of the 1990s and, a bit later, the heirloom farming, locavore, and slow food movements that continue to this day, through farmers' markets, local restaurants, and home kitchens. The hippies were doing it first — or again — with their new attitudes about living and eating in communal ways.

Many whole food and vegetarian cookbooks emerged during this time — *Tassajara Bread Book* by Zen priest Edward Espe Brown, *Recipes for Life* by Ann Wigmore, *The New York Times Natural Foods Cookbook* by Jean Hewitt, and *Moosewood Cookbook* by Mollie Katzen. I still look to these books today for practical advice and inspiration. The wisdom they contain is true, rooted in the same principles I learned in our garden: that food should be real, that beauty can be simple, that cooking is an act of love.

This appreciation for natural beauty and simple abundance was never more evident than in my mother's blackberry pie. Every time I make it now, I'm transported back to those Tennessee woods, to the patient act of picking berries with my brothers and her. Making a pie crust was more than a cooking lesson — it was a ritual, a meditation on transformation. The anticipation would build as the aroma filled our little home, and those piecrust scrap cookies she made to hold us over were more than just treats — they were her way of teaching us that love is in the details.

Mom's Blackberry Pie

This might be my best food memory of all time. Not just the pie itself, but the whole experience: picking berries with my brothers and mom, learning the sacred art of pie crust, the anticipation building as the aroma filled our home. Even those little piecrust scrap cookies dusted with cinnamon sugar were part of the magic. All of this, surrounded by those beautiful woods in our little home on a mountain in the Cumberland Gap of middle Tennessee — there couldn't be anything more perfect than that.

Ingredients:

1 quart blackberries, fresh picked if you have access

¾ cups granulated sugar

1 tsp. vanilla extract

⅛ tsp. ground clove

⅛ tsp. ground allspice

⅛ tsp. ground cinnamon

4 Tbsp. cornstarch

Zest of 1 lemon

Juice of 1 lemon, seeds removed (zest first, then juice)

1 large egg white, whisked until just blended

Salt

Directions:

Adjust rack to middle position and preheat oven to 375 degrees

Thoroughly rinse and dry blackberries

In large bowl, whisk together sugar, cornstarch, spices and salt

Add blackberries and gently toss with clean hands until coated

Add lemon juice, toss again until sugar has dissolved and berries start to macerate

Pour filling into chilled pie crust (raw, not blind baked)

Top with second crust and trim excess ½ inch larger than the crimped edge

Tuck crust into edge of bottom crust and crimp

Make about 6 slit incisions with sharp paring knife in flower petal design

Brush top with egg white and dust with 1 Tbsp. granulated sugar

Bake at 375 degrees for approximately 50 minutes, turning halfway through, until juices bubble and crust is golden brown

---

Years later, when I was in college, my parents went on an eight-week summer adventure exploring the great Northwest. They asked me to take care of the house, the pets, and — most importantly — the garden. Although they planned to be gone through July and August, my mother had started a full garden out of habit, just as she had for the previous fifteen years. I was working at a cool restaurant called Hawkeye's in Knoxville at the time, earning extra money while attending the University of Tennessee. Being interested in food and cooking, I was more than happy to tend Mom's garden. Little did I know what I was walking into.

Mom asked me to keep up with everything — plants watered, tomatoes and squash picked and "put up," as folks say in the South. She asked that I pick the ripe tomatoes and simply freeze them whole. This was my first revelation about tomatoes — that they could be preserved so simply. She explained that freezing them whole would make them easy to can upon her return.

But let me suggest one of the best things you should do if you ever encounter a row of homegrown killer tomatoes. On a hot, sunny day, find the biggest, ripest tomato you can. Pick it, and maybe grab a few leaves of basil while you're at it (a good gardener would have planted both for the summer). Quickly take it inside and don't wait to use it. Slice about three thick slices while it's still warm. Throw them on a plate and sprinkle them with some sea salt and the basil leaves. Eat them while they're still warm from the sun. It is the closest to tasting the very idea of freshness you will ever come. Or, even better, make a sun-warmed tomato sandwich — a couple of thick slices of just-picked ripe tomato, some white bread, mayonnaise, and sea salt is all you'll need for this simple delight.

She also asked that I shred as many ripe zucchini as possible using a food processor, freezing the squash in airtight baggies. "Since you like to cook," she added, "use the fresh vegetables any way you want. Make fresh tomato salsa, gazpacho, marinara — freeze them or use them as you please. Just please keep up and don't let things go to waste."

Within days of their leaving, I got to work. I checked the tomato row and gathered about ten ripe tomatoes, found three large zucchinis, along with some yellow hook-neck squash and fresh cucumbers. Easy enough, I thought. I used some for my supper and let the others sit in a bowl on the kitchen table, a still-life painting come to life.

The next day I did the same, and the day after that I made some fresh tomato salsa. A few days later, I started freezing the tomatoes as directed — there were too many for my immediate use. I made zucchini bread and shredded then froze the leftovers as asked. This became the routine, but as the weeks passed, it became clear that this was no simple task — this was a real job.

One day, after about four days of neglect, I picked an entire wheelbarrow of different veggies. The garden's abundance had become almost comical. I made a four-gallon pot of marinara and several loaves of zucchini bread. I froze about twenty tomatoes, about twenty-five ears worth of corn, and more shredded zucchini than I could count. I started to give baskets of vegetables to my friends' families and to neighbors. They were happy to take them off my hands, but still the garden produced more.

I was shocked by the sheer volume the garden yielded that summer. I filled up the chest freezer, made pickles, canned salsas, stewed tomatoes, and now I must confess I even started to throw some straight into the compost instead of using them. I promise I did my best. But I learned so much about gardens that summer, especially that one person only needs about four tomato plants and one or two summer squash. Still, I loved having all that bulk for my personal use, though a couple of times I did consider taking a cross to hold up to that garden and asking the garden gods to have some sympathy.

Here's my favorite way to honor those incredible tomatoes, a recipe that celebrates their natural perfection:

Homegrown Tomato & Basil Sauce

This is my favorite easy tomato sauce recipe for homegrown tomatoes. It works beautifully over angel hair pasta with nothing but Parmesan cheese. The method of removing the skins is part of the French process called concassé — a technique that respects the tomato's perfect flesh while removing its bitter skin.

Ingredients:

8 large homegrown tomatoes or heirloom tomatoes
3 cloves of garlic, peeled
1 cup red or white wine
12 fresh basil leaves
2 tsp. kosher salt
¼ tsp. ground black pepper
2 trays or 1 quart ice cubes for ice bath

Directions:

In a large sauce pot bring 2 quarts of water to a boil

Remove the core from each tomato, leaving it intact

Turn tomatoes upside down onto cutting board and score bottom of each with a 2-inch X mark with paring knife, only skin deep

Prepare ice bath in large mixing bowl with ice cubes and 1 quart tap water

When water reaches rapid boil, carefully lower 2 - 3 tomatoes into water

Blanch for about 1½ minutes until skins start to fall off

Transfer each tomato with slotted spoon to ice bath

Repeat with remaining tomatoes

Remove skins, which will easily fall off

Chop skinned tomatoes into quarters

Add tomatoes, garlic, wine, salt and pepper to medium saucepan

Cook on medium-low heat for 40 minutes

Let cool until room temperature

Add basil and blend until smooth

Strain through screen strainer or chinois to remove seeds

Serve over angel hair pasta, gnocchi, or use in lasagna or eggplant parmesan

---

That summer of killer tomatoes taught me something important about beauty — sometimes it comes in overwhelming abundance, and part of creating beauty is learning to manage it, to share it, to let it flow through you to others. Those endless tomatoes weren't just fruit to be harvested; they were lessons in generosity, in community, in the cycle of growth and sharing that would shape my later life as a chef.

Today, when I tend my own small garden or visit farmers' markets, I think back to that summer. I remember the weight of those warm tomatoes in my hands, the satisfaction of filling freezers and pantries, the joy of sharing with neighbors. The "plastic fantastic" world my parents had rejected was all about convenience, about disconnection from the source of our food. But in that Tennessee garden, I learned that real food — like real beauty — requires attention, care, and sometimes can be a little overwhelming.

The garden taught me that nature's abundance can't always be contained in neat rows or perfect plans. Sometimes it spills over, demands more of us than we expected, forces us to adapt and share and grow. These lessons would serve me well in the years to come, as I made my way from that Tennessee mountainside to professional kitchens, always seeking to create beauty from whatever the season provided.

Looking back now, I realize that summer wasn't just about managing an overwhelming harvest — it was about learning to embrace abundance in all its forms. Those "killer tomatoes" were teaching me that beauty, like love, multiplies when shared. It's a lesson I carry with me still, whether I'm cooking for friends, setting a table, or simply admiring a perfectly ripe tomato, warm from the sun.

Finding My Way to Fancy

Something I grew up with that seems to have faded over the years is one of life's greatest inventions: the potluck party. These gatherings happened constantly among my parents' friends during my childhood, and they taught me my first lessons about how sharing food could create community. Today, reviving this tradition has become one of my life's missions. It's also given me the perfect excuse to collect vintage Pyrex, Tupperware, and fancy warming plates — though back then, I didn't realize my love for these beautiful serving pieces was another early sign of who I was becoming.

For the past decade, I've thrown my own annual holiday soirée. I've heard the invitation is coveted by some, or at least I like to think so. I've learned that the secret is to spend all your time creating the ambiance and minimal time on the food. I make one spectacular element — a beautiful punch in a vintage bowl adorned with hooks for crystal cups, with an old-school ice ring floating artfully within. It's the kind of detail that transforms a gathering into an occasion.

A punch is more than just a drink — it's a centerpiece, a conversation starter, a way of saying "this moment matters." When I make punch for a party, it's always the last thing I do before guests arrive. Often, I wait until the first knock at the door. This isn't laziness — it's timing. You don't want the ice to melt before the party starts. This attention to detail, this understanding that presentation matters as much as taste, was something I understood instinctively even as a child, though I didn't always feel free to express it.

Here's my favorite punch recipe, one that embodies this philosophy of making everyday moments special:

Poached Pear and Port Wine Punch

Ingredients:

1 750 ml bottle of Port wine (doesn't need to be expensive)
3 fresh pears (any variety, but Red Anjous preferred)
2 oranges, sliced into ¼-inch disks (reserve 5 disks for garnish)
1 vanilla bean, sliced in half lengthwise
2 whole star anise
7 whole allspice berries
7 whole cloves
2 cinnamon sticks
2 bay leaves
1 cup granulated sugar
2 bottles of Prosecco or Cava
3 cans or bottles of ginger beer
4½ cups aged Caribbean rum
Ice ring with cranberries (see notes)

Directions:

Peel the pears, leaving stems intact if possible

Combine pears, sugar, vanilla bean halves, orange disks (saving 5 for garnish), whole spices, bay leaves and port wine in large saucepan

Bring to simmer over high heat

Reduce heat to medium-low and simmer 30 minutes

Remove from heat and cool to room temperature

Once cooled, discard cinnamon sticks and orange slices but leave remaining spices

Remove poached pears and cut in half lengthwise

Place ice ring in punch bowl

Pour Prosecco and ginger beer over ice

Add rum

Carefully pour the spiced poaching liquid into the bowl and stir gently

Float pear halves and remaining orange slices on surface

Serve immediately

There's something magical about a properly prepared punch bowl, especially during the holiday season. I learned early that a beautiful presentation doesn't have to be complicated — it just needs to be thoughtful. The ice ring isn't just functional; it's decorative, a way of turning necessity into art. My grandmother would make the ice ring with Kool-Aid for color, but I prefer adding cranberries or herbs for a more sophisticated effect. It's about elevating the simple into the special, something I've been doing since I was old enough to reach the kitchen counter.

Something I've learned from years of hosting: the main idea is to spend your energy creating the ambiance, not stressing over elaborate food. My holiday parties now follow a simple formula — I provide the punch and the atmosphere, my guests bring food and champagne. It's wildly festive, and there's always too much to eat. Many of my guests go into a mild panic or competition mode when it comes to their covered dish, though I always wonder why everyone's so nervous about making a casserole. I've heard it's because some are afraid to cook for a professional chef, but I think it's because the guest list is full of LGBTQ+ overachievers, each bringing their own beautiful way of showing love through food.

This tendency to impress means we get far more than just casseroles. A beautiful home-smoked whole salmon with all the accoutrements appears on the main table every year, courtesy of my friend John. Alongside it, you'll find Dylan's melting snowman dip, which is both whimsical and sophisticated — exactly the kind of unexpected delight that makes a party memorable.

My longtime friend Dylan has been bringing this to my holiday parties for years, and it's become a beloved tradition. The snowman always melts morbidly in the dish, causing quite a stir among the guests. There are usually more pictures of that snowman on social media the next day than any other aspect of the party — before and after shots that tell the story of the evening.

Dylan always makes sure to turn the snowman's frown upside down once it's fully melted. While this dish isn't a complexly flavored culinary feat, it's something more valuable — it's fun, memorable, and it gets people talking. Sometimes Dylan freezes cubes of picante sauce and places them in the center of the cheese balls, causing an even more dramatic effect while adding unexpected flavor. It's precisely this kind of creative thinking that transforms a simple party dish into performance art.

Dylan's Melting Snowman Dip

Ingredients:

1 32 oz. package of Velveeta Queso Blanco or original

1 lb. cream cheese spread

1 large pointy carrot for hat and eyes

2 black olive slices for eyes

1 red bell pepper slice for the mouth

1 green bell pepper for a cut out bow

2 pretzel sticks for arms

1 toothpick

1 small can Sterno fuel lamp

1 3-quart chafing dish

Directions:

With clean hands form the cold Velveeta into 3 balls: a large, a medium and one small for the head

With a rubber spatula spread the cream cheese spread in a ¼-inch layer over the entirety of each cheese ball

Place separated on a tray in the refrigerator while creating the decorations

For the carrot hat and nose, cut off a ⅛ inch disk-shaped slice from the larger end, then cut a 2-inch section from the middle

Fashion the disk onto the bottom and attach with a toothpick to look like a top hat

Cut off 2 inches of the pointy end for the nose and set aside

Cut out 1 thin sliver of red bell pepper for the mouth and cut a 2-inch bow shape out of the flattest part of the green bell pepper

To assemble, place the cream cheese-covered cheese balls with the largest one in the center of the chafing dish

Add medium sized ball firmly on top of the largest one, then the smallest one firmly atop the medium ball for the head

Place the carrot top hat firmly atop his head and decorate with remaining features

Place chafing dish carefully on the buffet table

Place a bowl of corn chips on the side

Place the Sterno can according to proper slot under the chafing dish

Wait for guests to arrive before lighting

Watch it slowly melt and use the chips for dipping

I also decorate my place extravagantly for the holidays. It's a small condo in a quirky old high-rise in downtown Atlanta, barely big enough for fifteen people, but somehow, I manage to squeeze in fifty or so guests, packed like fancy sardines. Over the years, I've learned that the key to managing a crowd in a small space isn't just about arrangement — it's about creating multiple centers of interest that naturally distribute people throughout your home.

One of my favorite space-management techniques is turning my bedroom into a crafting room during parties. The bed becomes a crafting table (best to use a bedspread you're not too precious about — glitter has a way of becoming permanent decor). I cover it with decorative trays, cups, and bowls filled with crafting supplies: glue guns, scissors, sequins, felt, feathers, and pipe cleaners. This isn't just about utilizing space — it's about creating an experience, giving people permission to play and create.

A friend took this idea and adapted it for their own party, setting up sock puppet-making stations. The best pictures and stories always come from these craft rooms. It's a perfect icebreaker, getting people out of their shells while literally getting them out of the crowded main rooms. I encourage guests to create ornaments during holiday parties, but it could be any kind of craft any time of year. By the end of the night, my house is covered in beautiful and sometimes inappropriate handmade art pieces — and glitter, always glitter. I leave them up until I take down all the holiday decorations. These crafts make my home feel warm and personal during the rest of the season, and many make it onto the tree year after year. Some pieces are so clever they stay up permanently, becoming part of my home's evolving story.

I've been hosting dinner and cocktail parties, large and small, for as long as I can remember. They started modest and grew more elaborate over the years — you could say they were the beginning of my "fanciness." Like any skill, hosting takes a mixture of natural inclination and learned experience. My first soirée didn't go off without a hitch, nor did my second or third. In fact, it took years before I truly mastered what I now call "the salon."

The salon, an Italian invention of the 16th century that has spread worldwide, is a gathering where guests amuse one another through conversation. The cardinal rule of any memorable get-together is the guest list — it's about creating the perfect mixture of personalities and perspectives. I've read countless books and watched hundreds of shows about entertaining. Over time, I've collected ideas like I collect serving pieces, keeping what works and gracefully retiring what doesn't.

I've learned to invite people from different backgrounds, cultures, professions, and talents. You don't want all introverts or all extroverts; you need a balance of creative types and analytical minds, doctors and designers, bartenders and writers. It's essential to add "fresh meat" — new faces who can bring different perspectives to mix with guests who've been attending for years.

I've discovered that some guests should know each other, while others shouldn't — the friction between familiar and unfamiliar creates energy, sparks conversation. Over time, I've identified what I call my "forever guests" — those certain people everyone finds intriguing, who keep conversation flowing without letting it become too serious. They become part of the gathering's foundation, acting almost as built-in social facilitators.

But even the perfect guest list needs the right setting. I've learned that lighting is everything. The best thing one can do to create ambiance is to set the mood with low lighting. While I love real flame candles, I've begun leaning toward electric ones for practicality. The trick is to have one or two real candles in prominent positions and then use electric ones concealed in decorative votive holders throughout the space. Place the flame-lit candles where they'll be noticed and tuck the electric ones into opaque holders. This creates the sensation that they're all real while maintaining safety and convenience.

Another lighting tip: if possible, have guests arrive around sunset. This "golden hour" makes everything and everyone look magical, especially depending on which direction your windows face. But have your dimmed lights and candles ready as darkness falls. Before the invention of smart lighting, I would switch out all the bulbs in my home with the lowest wattage I could find — 15 watts, and the ever-elusive 7½-watt bulbs were my favorites. Nothing higher than 25 watts or its equivalent. With the right lighting, guests don't notice the crack in the mirror, the missing piece of molding that's been bothering you, or the baseboards you haven't had time to fix.

For dinner parties, I usually provide a couple of simple hors d'oeuvres, laid out just before arrival time in a spot away from where I'm finishing the main courses. I've learned to use what I already have: slice and toast bread that needs to be used, blend olives with herbs from the garden, put out some cheese. A can of smoked oysters or roasted peppers kept on hand can elevate the simplest crackers. Or arrange olives and nuts on a beautiful serving tray with quick-pickled vegetables and herb garnishes. The key is to make it look intentional, not thrown together — presentation transforms the ordinary into the special.

I always set a proper table. To me, a beautiful table setting is the epitome of being fancy. Don't be afraid to use "the good stuff" — if you don't use it for a party, when will you use it? Being the maximalist that I am, I'm always collecting interesting serving pieces, glassware, trays, charcuterie boards, and table linens. If you're a minimalist, at least have one or two really nice serving pieces you can rely on. I have several sets of china passed down to me, and I use them all. My friends lovingly call my style "old lady chic," and I wear that title with pride.

When I'm making everything for a party — the place settings, flower arrangements, entertainment, food — one of my favorite ways to ease the pressure is to ask a cocktail-loving guest to bring a pre-batched drink for everyone. I find out what they're bringing and have a clean bar with ice and all necessary tools ready, including their requested glassware. This works beautifully for non-alcoholic options too. The key is asking someone who's reliably punctual, preferably willing to arrive twenty minutes early. When you can offer drinks without having to stop and make them yourself, you're free to help with coats, arrange dishes guests bring, and most importantly, be present with your guests.

Here's a favorite of mine on the cocktail front:

The "Road Less Traveled" Cocktail

This is a simple twist on a Boulevardier Cocktail, substituting Aperol for Campari and using orange peel instead of lemon. Expressing the orange peel might seem excessive, but it's crucial for balance. The oil mist that forms on the surface adds complexity through aroma. Our olfactory sense is vital to taste — this is why bartenders clap herbs between their hands before garnishing.

Ingredients:

2 oz. rye

1 oz. Aperol

1 oz. Sweet Vermouth

Orange peel

Ice

King cube (if available)

Tools:

Mixing glass

Cocktail spoon

Jigger

Cocktail strainer

Peeler

Old Fashioned glass (rocks glass)

Directions:

Fill Old Fashioned glass with ice to chill while building cocktail

Add 1 cup ice to mixing glass or tin

Pour rye, Aperol and sweet vermouth over ice

Stir vigorously with cocktail spoon for 30-45 seconds

Discard ice from old fashioned glass

Add king cube to glass (or about 6 regular cubes)

Carefully strain chilled spirits over cube

Make 2½-inch swath of orange peel with peeler

Hold peel skin-down over cocktail, pinch to express oils. Repeat once

Rub peel along rim, form into twist and place atop glass

The week I turned six, my understanding of what a party could be changed forever. My mom took me to the "big" grocery store in our little town — though it was actually quite small by today's standards, unless you wanted to drive 30 miles to something larger. It was the middle of June, and being out of school for summer break gave me that delicious feeling of endless possibility. My attitude toward school at that age was very "out of sight, out of mind." I would practically forget school existed during summer break. I didn't have a care in the world, and better yet, my birthday was just around the corner.

That day, mom told me I could pick out one special item of my choice from the store.

This was a big deal in our health-conscious household. While friends' pantry cupboards were stuffed with five or six boxes of Fruity Pebbles, Sugar Pops, and Cocoa Puffs, our cabinets held Grape Nuts and generic puffed rice. In my desire to be just like the other kids, this seemed like my big chance to finally obtain my very own box of Lucky Charms, with its fancy shaped pastel marshmallows and bright-eyed leprechaun.

To my young mind, this was the grossest, craziest, most sugary antithesis to our usual breakfast fare — and therefore perfect. The TV ads made it look like the most amazing thing a kid could ever hope for. But when I finally tried it, it was just ... okay. The sugar rush was disappointingly short-lived. I ate most of the dried-up marshmallows first and wanted nothing to do with the rest. It certainly didn't live up to the Leprechaun's promise of being "magically delicious."

While I was contemplating cereals, I ran into my parents' friend, Martee. My mother had told me earlier that week that I could have a birthday party and invite the friends of my choice. So right there in the cereal aisle, I proudly informed Martee of the upcoming celebration and told her that she and her husband Jamie were invited. Moments later, I found my mother in the baking aisle talking to another family friend, Geno. I handed her my selected box of cereal — hoping she'd be properly horrified — then proceeded to invite Geno to the party as well.

My mom asked, "Oh, you want Geno to come to your birthday party?" I reminded her that she had given me permission to make my own guest list. She said she thought the list would be made up of my friends. "But Mom," I said, "Geno is our friend." She shrugged and agreed, just as Martee rounded the corner. After greetings, Martee informed my mother that she too was invited to my party and checked that it was okay. My mom, looking surprised, said "Well, I guess I did say you could have whoever you wanted."

They all laughed at my precocious party planning, and Mom gave them the details. As we completed our errands that day and throughout the week leading up to the party, I continued inviting our family friends and their families. It became an inside joke among the adults that I was so forward in inviting so many grown-ups, but it seemed perfectly natural to me. These were the people who made life interesting, who brought different perspectives and stories to our gatherings. I had experienced many potlucks and gatherings with numerous attendees growing up at our home, so why should my birthday party be any different?

I remember being thrilled whenever we had get-togethers at our house. My mom would ask me to make "no smoking" signs and directions to the bathroom, which I gladly created with my 64-piece Crayola crayon set (the one with the built-in sharpener on the back!) I made decorations and picked flowers for the table. But my greatest honor was being asked to arrange the cheese and cracker trays. Having my mom trust me with this task felt like recognition of my platter-arranging skills, which she had so carefully taught me. I would spend ages working on them, fanning out the assorted crackers, layering the cheese slices, and garnishing them with sprays of parsley.

My sixth birthday party grew into something much bigger than anyone expected. In addition to several of my classroom besties, I had invited at least two dozen adults. My parents bought beer for the grown-ups, and the children churned ice cream with a hand-cranked machine on the back porch under my uncle's supervision. It was one of those manual machines that required you to sit on it with a towel between your bottom and the freezing-cold ice while turning the handle as fast as you could. Exhausting but magical — we all took turns churning, making the ice cream a communal creation.

But what I remember most about this birthday wasn't the ice cream or even the guests — it was my mom's strawberry shortcake. She had made this delightful dessert just two weeks earlier when strawberries were coming into season, and it was the best thing I'd tasted in my young life. I quickly requested it again for my birthday. Although my mom called them "strawberry shortcakes," they were actually lightly sweetened buttermilk biscuits split in half and filled with homemade strawberry sauce and whipped cream. This was how her grandmother made them, and now she was passing this tradition to me.

Mom made enough sweet biscuits for everyone at the party, each one slathered with peak-of-the-season, locally picked strawberries. The berries were macerated in sugar and vanilla until they turned into a bright, syrupy red sauce. A big dollop of whipped cream and a generous scoop of our hand-cranked ice cream — both homemade — crowned each serving. I requested this "cake" for my birthday for many years after, proud to have something so unique and special instead of a store-bought cake in a box.

I don't want to get into the classic battle of what is — and what isn't — a proper shortcake, but I've always preferred the biscuit over the traditional sponge cake often used in shortcake recipes. For the past twenty years, I've made these "shortbiscuits" every June. I've also served them as a spring menu item at several restaurants where

I've been a chef. Like so many things I love, timing is everything — strawberries are always better when eaten during their peak season. I typically don't use them when they aren't at their best. That goes for most fruits and vegetables as well. Just like tomatoes, avocados, peaches, or any other produce, they are always best when used at their peak ripeness, purchased from a local supplier if you can't pick them yourself.

Looking back at that sixth birthday party, I can see now how it was more than just a celebration — it was my first real attempt at creating a gathering that crossed boundaries of age and expectation. These biscuits aren't just a recipe passed down through generations; they're a testament to choosing your own way of doing things. A regular birthday cake would have been easier, more "normal," but even then, I was drawn to making things special, making them fancy.

My mom's version of strawberry shortcake, with the buttermilk sweet biscuit used in place of a sponge cake, is what her mom made for her ... and so on. It's a delightful way to use leftover biscuits, which I'm sure is how this dish originated, but they're so special they're worth making on their own. This is the perfect way to feature the berries that let you know summer is just around the corner. (Try this recipe with blackberries, blueberries, or raspberries later in the summer.)

Mom's Strawberry "Shortbiscuits"

Ingredients for the macerated strawberries:

16 oz. container of fresh strawberries (or 1 lb.)
¾ cup granulated sugar
1½ tsp. vanilla extract

Ingredients for the Biscuits:

2 cups self-rising baking flour (White Lily brand recommended)
1 stick unsalted butter (cold)
2 Tbsp. melted butter (for brushing)
3 Tbsp. granulated sugar
½ tsp. salt
1 Tbsp. baking powder
1 cup + 2 Tbsp. buttermilk
Extra flour for patting and cutting the biscuits

Ingredients for the orange honey whipped cream:

1 pint heavy (whipping) cream
½ tsp. vanilla extract
¼ cup orange blossom honey

Directions for the macerated strawberries:

Clean the strawberries by floating them in a large mixing bowl of cold water.

Allow them to float and stir around with your hands to let the silt and dirt from the strawberries fall to the bottom.

Transfer the berries to a strainer by lifting them gently from the water, so as to not disturb the silt on the bottom.

With a paring knife slice off as little of the top off as possible, removing only the green part of the strawberries.

Laying the flat cut part of the berries side down on a cutting board, slice the berries into quarters from top to bottom.

Place the clean cut strawberries and ¾ cups of granulated sugar and vanilla extract in a small saucepan. Then place the pan on medium-high heat.

Bring the strawberries to a simmer, stirring occasionally.

Once the berries have just come to a simmer and sugar has dissolved, immediately remove them from the heat. Transfer them to a mixing bowl and place in the refrigerator to cool (or place them over an ice bath in a metal bowl to cool more quickly.)

To make the Biscuits:

Preheat the oven to 365 degrees and adjust the oven rack to the middle position. (If you have a convection oven use convection mode, but it is not necessary.)

Before you start this recipe, I find it is best to create clean floured workspace to cut the biscuits. Clean a 12 inch x 12 inch counter space and dust it lightly with flour. Also have your baking sheet out and a 2½ inch biscuit cutter out and ready (or a straight edged juice glass will work for cutting the biscuits.) Place 2 cups of self-rising flour in a large mixing bowl.

Add the salt, baking powder and 2 Tbsp. granulated sugar and mix with a wire whisk until well blended. (Reserve 1 Tbsp. of the sugar for dusting the biscuits prior to baking.)

With a pastry cutter or your hands "cut" the cold butter into the mixture by pressing it into the flour and mixing it between your fingers or the pastry cutter blades until it has formed into clumpy pea-size bits. The pieces do not need to be perfect in size or conformity. Do not over mix.

The dough should be crumbly and falling apart in a meal-like fashion.

Next create a small well in the center of the mixture with your hands and pour 1 cup of buttermilk into the well.

Quickly but gently mix the buttermilk into the flour and butter mixture with your hands until it just comes together. It will be a little loose and slightly heavy in your hands, and very wet and sticky. If the dough feels dry add a little more buttermilk. (up to 2 Tbsp.)

Gently pat it into a ball and transfer it to the floured work surface.

Try to remove as much of the dough from your hands and add it to the dough, then thoroughly clean your hands with soap and hot water to remove excess. Toss a little more flour over the top of the ball and gently pat it down to about 1½ inches in height and round. It is okay if the edges of the dough have large cracks.

Flour the biscuit cutter or edge of the glass. Press the cutter or glass into the dough straight down in a quick motion and place each biscuit onto an un-greased baking sheet about 1 inch apart.

Re-form the scrap leftover pieces of dough and pat out again to 1½ inches and cut more biscuits with a floured cutter or juice glass. Repeat this until there is not enough remaining dough to make another biscuit (approximately 6 - 8 biscuits.)

Brush tops lightly with melted butter and then give them a light dusting with the remaining tablespoon of granulated sugar.

Place the tray on the middle rack of the pre-heated oven and bake at 365 degrees for 12 – 15 minutes or until starting to turn golden brown. Turn the tray once halfway through the baking time to help them bake evenly. (If using a convection oven, you may need to reduce the cooking slightly.)

Transfer the biscuits with a spatula to a cooling rack.

The biscuits will still have a soft center at first and will finish upon cooling.

For the whipped cream:

Add the 1 pint heavy cream to the bowl of a stand mixer fitted with a wire whip (or a large mixing bowl and hand mixer will suffice.)

Next add the vanilla extract and the orange blossom honey.

Start mixing on low speed then as it thickens, adjust the speed to medium and then eventually high speed.

Whip the cream until soft peaks form and the cream sticks to the whip or beaters (about 3½ – 4 minutes.)

When I think back to the memory of this first "soirée" — my birthday party where I got to choose the guests and the "cake" — I see now it was the beginning of my desire to have a hand in all aspects of entertaining, especially the food. Starting with my sixth birthday, and continuing through the years, I learned to keep the guest list interesting. Don't hold back, as a celebration is only as good as its attendees. Even then, I understood that the best gatherings mix different kinds of people, different generations, different perspectives.

I also learned the importance of serving homemade, seasonal foods with local ingredients, and sharing your family's traditions. Each strawberry shortbiscuit was more than just dessert — it was a way of saying "this moment matters enough to do it properly." I'm grateful my family showed me how to throw a party while letting me be myself. They taught me not to believe everything I saw on TV (thanks, Lucky Charms!), and showed me we didn't need artificial luxuries to have full lives.

What's so much better than a box of overly sugared, tooth-rotting cereal? Or a Betty Crocker-mix cake? Or, worse yet, a grocery store cake? The answer is simple: strawberries and biscuits, homemade whipped cream, and hand-cranked ice cream. I believe this not just because it's what I grew up with, but because I've never found anything better. And what's so much better than the plastic trinket found in the bottom of a box of Lucky Charms? A real experience — a soirée with people you love, and a family that teaches you how to create moments worth remembering.

These early lessons in entertaining weren't just about food or guest lists — they were about having the courage to do things your own way. Whether it was inviting adults to a child's birthday party, choosing shortbiscuits over traditional cake, or spending time arranging cheese trays "just so," I was learning to trust my instincts about what makes a gathering special. These seemingly small choices were actually early expressions of who I was becoming — someone who would always choose the fancy path, even when it wasn't the obvious one.

Today, when I host parties in my Atlanta home, I think back to that six-year-old boy, proudly inviting grown-ups to his birthday party, insisting on strawberry shortbiscuits instead of cake. He knew something important: that celebrations aren't about following conventions — they're about creating beauty in your own way, about gathering people together and offering them something genuine, something special, something uniquely yours.

Real Men Do Indeed Eat Quiche

My first real job was working at my dad's restaurant, Shenanigans. It was a trendy college town deli and bar near campus, the kind of place where worlds collided — professors having lunch meetings, students nursing hangovers with coffee, locals coming in for what was, at the time, cutting-edge fare. I worked alongside college students — whom I greatly admired — my high school friend Lara, my brother Jay, and my dad. The menu offered sandwiches piled high with sliced meats, cheeses, and what were then exotic toppings like alfalfa sprouts. We served salads, bagels, pizzas, soft-serve frozen yogurt, and imported beer on tap. Before the craft brewery revolution, imported beer was what made you sophisticated.

One of my favorite menu items, the one I'd often choose for my shift — lunch — was a big slice of homemade quiche. We offered varieties that seemed revolutionary at the time — spinach and ham, mushroom and bacon, and my favorite: sweet onion, tomato and Swiss. Quiche was wildly popular then, though not everyone understood it. For those unfamiliar, it's essentially a savory egg custard and cheese filling in a flaky crust, with additions like cured meats, vegetables, and herbs. Simple but elegant — everything I loved about cooking.

I got paid extra to make the quiches, and I still make that tomato and sweet onion combination today. It's one of my favorite comfort foods, especially paired with a simple salad. Perfect to heat up the next day for breakfast or lunch. Now I use heirloom tomatoes and Gruyere cheese, and when Vidalia onions are in season, their sweetness creates something magical.

But making quiche in the early 1980s meant confronting more than just cooking techniques. There was this phrase going around: "Real men don't eat quiche." You'd hear it everywhere – it was on t-shirts, coffee mugs, dropped into casual conversation like a joke everyone was supposed to get. The phrase came from a book by the same name, a supposedly satirical "guidebook to all that is truly masculine." The author would later claim he didn't mean for it to be taken seriously. But it was. Of course it was.

I found the whole "real men don't eat quiche" phenomenon bewildering and, if I'm honest, painful. It carried that familiar tone I encountered in so many areas of my adolescent life – expressions and opinions that were meant to be "just jokes" but weren't funny at all. They always seemed to come at the expense of others, and very typically, effeminate boys. In those days, it was completely normal to throw around derogatory terms like "faggot," "queer bait," "bull-dyke," and "lesbo" in school halls, playgrounds, and popular movies. These words were repeated by my peers, and I would often pretend to laugh along to hide the real me.

The real me – the one who loved flower arranging, who had a passion for art and cooking, who found joy in things that weren't "acceptable" for a young boy to enjoy. And now here was quiche, somehow given a gender identity and randomly chosen to be labeled "unmasculine." The absurdity of it struck me even then: how could an innocent savory pastry be deemed unsuitable for men? Should pot-pie be off limits? Should "real men" stop eating doughnuts and croissants as well?

I thought to myself, if real men don't eat quiche, I don't want to be a "real man." This was a familiar sentiment that would surface again and again throughout my adolescent and young adult life. Each time I found myself drawn to something deemed too fancy, too feminine, too much, I had to choose between hiding my interests or facing the consequences of being different.

Working at Shenanigans became a kind of sanctuary. In the kitchen, making quiche became an act of quiet defiance. I took pride in crafting each one perfectly — the crust just right, the filling silky and properly seasoned. The deli existed in this wonderful in-between space: part of the conservative South but also a college town establishment where different ideas and ways of being were, if not always embraced, at least tolerated.

The irony wasn't lost on me that while some men were proudly proclaiming they didn't eat quiche, others — professors, students, businessmen — were regularly ordering it for lunch. They didn't seem concerned about their masculinity being threatened by eggs and pastry. This gave me hope, though I couldn't have articulated it then: there were different ways to be a man, different ways to move through the world.

Here's my favorite quiche recipe, one that honors both tradition and personal taste. It's a dish that taught me that sometimes the most powerful thing you can do is simply create beauty, regardless of what others might think:

Heirloom Tomato & Sweet Onion Quiche

This recipe is more than just a dish — it's a statement about the arbitrary nature of gender roles and the universal appeal of good food. While some might still raise an eyebrow at a man making quiche, I've found that skepticism tends to disappear with the first bite.

This recipe works particularly well with fresh heirloom tomatoes at their peak. The key is letting the custard set properly before slicing. Also, a great dish to make the night ahead for breakfast or brunch — it keeps very well in the refrigerator and easily reheats covered at 275 degrees for 20 minutes.

Ingredients:

1 large or 2 smaller heirloom tomatoes, any variety you prefer
1 small Vidalia, Walla Walla or Maui onion
1 9-inch pie crust (homemade or store-bought)
¾ cup fresh grated Gruyere cheese
¼ cup grated Parmesan
1½ cups heavy cream or half & half
3 large eggs
1 small garlic clove, minced
¼ tsp. curry powder
¾ inch of the top of a rosemary spring, chopped

1 tsp. fresh tarragon, chopped

2 sprigs of fresh thyme, chopped

¼ tsp. dried or fresh chopped dill

¼ tsp. grated nutmeg

1½ tsp. kosher salt

¼ tsp. fresh ground black peppercorn

Directions:

Keep the pie crust refrigerated until ready to fill. If using frozen store-bought, allow to thaw slightly but keep cold.

Slice the sweet onion into ⅛ inch thin slices.

Sauté the onions in a little butter over high heat until slightly soft, about 2 minutes. Set aside to cool.

Core the tomatoes and slice into ⅓ inch disks, then cut each disk in half making half- moon shapes.

Whisk eggs in a large mixing bowl for about 1 minute until well blended and lightly fluffy.

Add cream, spices, herbs, garlic, pepper and salt.

Mix into the custard with the whisk until well blended.

Add grated cheeses to bottom of pie crust and distribute evenly. Press down lightly.

Sprinkle sautéed onions over cheese evenly.

Carefully pour the custard mixture over onions and cheese.

Float tomato half-slices around the top in a pinwheel pattern.

Sprinkle a pinch of grated nutmeg over the top.

Place quiche on a sheet tray and bake at 350 degrees for approximately 45 minutes or until lightly browned on top and no longer jiggly.

Let cool for 15 minutes before serving to allow proper setting.

What started as a summer job at my father's restaurant over several years evolved into a career, though not without complications. My experience at Shenanigans led me to other jobs while studying art in college, then into early adulthood. I became a self-taught chef, cutting my teeth in my first real fine dining establishment, Hawkeye's, just up from the main strip in Knoxville while attending the University of Tennessee.

A bit later, once in Atlanta, I first encountered the complex dynamics of professional kitchens. The front of house was often staffed by gay servers and bartenders — a revelation to me. I had never before been surrounded by such an openly queer group of people.

They taught me, through their very existence, that it was possible to be proud of one's queerness. If you were a straight server, you pretty much had to be on board, since you were usually outnumbered by the queer staff members.

The kitchen, however, was a different world entirely — predominantly straight men, with an air of machismo that felt suffocating. From the beginning of my culinary career all the way until I left the industry during the COVID pandemic, derogatory and sexualized language aimed at gay and female kitchen staff was commonplace. We never had HR departments to guide us, but if we had, many would not have survived professionally.

Despite feeling at home with the front-of-house staff, I often felt pressure to "fit in with the guys" in the kitchen. This meant going along with the jeering and homophobia, laughing at jokes that cut too close to home. The behavior came from the top down, creating a fraternity-style atmosphere of hazing. Women were rare in the kitchen in those days, unless they were immigrant dishwashers, prep staff, or sometimes relegated to the salad station. Sometimes pastry chefs were women, but due to space restrictions, they often worked when the rest of the staff was absent.

Throughout my years in the industry, I worked with only a handful of female and queer line-cooks and back-of-house managers, compared to scores of straight males in those same positions. We queer back-of-the-house folk were definitely a rare breed, and we faced constant undermining. The straight male cooks and kitchen managers treated non-straight, non-male staff as if we simply weren't capable of doing the same job. We were called too sensitive, bitchy, weak, even too silly for the tough line of work — and believe me, it was tough. But everyone who ended up in the kitchen had earned their spot, often working twice as hard to prove themselves worthy despite the constant stream of derogatory language and disrespectful behavior.

During those years, inappropriate touching and sexual innuendos were handed out as freely as side orders. One owner in particular made a habit of undermining my authority in front of the kitchen staff, dismissing my objections as me being an overly sensitive "homo." He would mock other gay men and women who worked as servers, expecting me to join in the laughter. "The gays love me," he would chortle, waiting for my complicity. Not laughing would put you on his bad list, and I would hear through the grapevine later that he was asking, "What's up his ass?" and "Can't he take a joke?"

I experienced the same bias about being "overly emotional" that so many women have endured for far too long. Being in charge as head chef meant keeping the kitchen running like a well-oiled machine during the most hectic hours. The only way to command what we called "being in the trenches" was to be tough. But my toughness was often misinterpreted as emotional hysteria — something the straight male managers and chefs never had to deal with.

When I needed to be stern, it was often dismissed as me being "in a mood" or, as I'd overhear, that I "hadn't gotten laid lately." My authority would be undermined in front of the kitchen staff, and any protest was characterized as typical gay dramatics. Trust me — the gays did *not* love that owner, but we thought we had to put up with it. The fear of losing one's job for being "difficult" was a constant concern for gay and female employees.

Yet somehow, this treatment made me stronger rather than weaker. It wasn't new territory — while enduring workplace discrimination, I often flashed back to the harassment I'd faced in junior high P.E. classes and throughout high school. Each struggle became a lesson in resilience, each challenge an opportunity to prove that being queer and being capable were not mutually exclusive.

I eventually earned the respect I deserved from the kitchens I ran, and I aimed to change how we all were treated. This was the school of hard knocks, and it taught me to be tough when needed while remaining true to myself. The very qualities that made me a target — my attention to detail, my aesthetic sense, my emotional intelligence — became strengths that set my kitchens apart.

Looking back, I'm not sure what it was about Atlanta kitchens during those days, or if it was just those particular ones, but the machismo was rampant. Television didn't help — celebrity chefs were becoming household names, many of them reinforcing toxic masculinity with their aggressive personalities and "man food" focus. There were chefs yelling "Bam!" and Food Network stars claiming the art of testosterone-ridden bacon burgers and roadside diner meals "made for a man." Even a famous Italian TV chef, so well-loved, was only discarded by pop culture after the discovery of his sexual abuse of women in the workplace.

But there were bright spots — havens of professionalism and respect that showed me a better way was possible. For three years, I worked at a well-known and beloved French bistro called Babette's Café. This magical place was run by two remarkable women: Marla was the owner and Kelly, the executive chef. In Kelly's kitchen, I learned not just the French art of pan sauces, braising, emulsions, browning butter, and deglazing, but also how a kitchen could be run with both excellence and humanity.

At Babette's, everyone was treated equally regardless of gender or sexual identity. For the first time since my days at my dad's deli and my college stint at Hawkeye's, I felt truly respected. The work atmosphere — respectful, invigorating, fun — was revolutionary to me. In other restaurants, I had been trained to ignore the front-of-house staff, to see them as the enemy, as incompetent. The front-of-house staff were typically handled with scare tactics and treated as lazy, stupid, or both.

But at Babette's, with Marla and Kelly at the helm, everything was different. Everyone was treated with dignity. Our input was expected, our grievances were heard. The time I spent there gave me a new vision of how kitchens could operate, and I carried this model with me when I left. When I went on to become executive chef at other restaurants, I made it my mission to hire a diverse kitchen staff. I came to see that those at the front-of-house weren't our adversaries but our partners in creating something special. The food, the service, and the atmosphere were all equally important — each element contributing to what I had always understood as "fancy."

Of course, it wasn't always smooth sailing. Not everyone was ready for change. I still encountered old-school owners and front-of-house managers who couldn't seem to put their misogyny, racism, and homophobia behind them. They appeared threatened by even the idea of equality in the workplace. But that didn't stop me from trying — and more often than not, succeeding.

Today, when I dine at better establishments, I see how much the work atmosphere has evolved. I observe more women and LGBTQ+ workers in kitchens, and a general sense of fair treatment for all people — conscious ownership, management, and staff. In private conversations, some of my favorite restaurant owners and staff members reflect on those oppressive old days, marveling at how much has changed. While it makes me happy to hear this, I know the old school way still exists somewhere, and not just in restaurants.

It was definitely a school of tough knocks, and it took tremendous strength to transcend the discrimination. Looking back on my years in the business, I find that 95 percent of my experience was positive. But that other 5 percent — the slurs casually thrown around, the physical intimidation, the constant need to prove myself — could be overwhelming. There were days when I'd go home and cry from frustration, nights when I questioned whether I could continue in this field I loved.

Yet the good far outweighed the bad. I worked with incredibly talented and clever people from both the back- and front-of-house. I learned from generous chefs who shared their knowledge freely, and eager young cooks determined to absorb every lesson. I met countless well-cultured customers from all walks of life, many of whom became friends. I was fortunate to learn from wine and spirit makers from around the globe, and how to source beautiful produce and meats from local farmers. I ate wonderful authentic food made by our immigrant employees and absorbed their culture as well.

It was the experience of a lifetime, filled with both beauty and challenge. There was so much joy in learning about food and providing it to others. But the problems I've spoken about did exist and continue to be a problem in many work environments. Since I bore witness, I feel it's my duty to shed light on them. These stories too often get swept under the rug, dismissed as "just the way things are." I can only hope that sharing them might help current and future staff and employers alike.

After leaving one particularly challenging restaurant position, I had dinner with one of my favorite longtime customers. He hadn't been in for some time, and when I reached out, I learned why. The story he shared crystallized everything I'd experienced in the industry. This customer's son is gay, and he would often bring his partner and their adopted boy to the restaurant. They were regulars, part of what made the place special. One evening, when my customer was trying to enjoy a meal with his girlfriend, the owner approached their table for what should have been friendly conversation. Instead, he walked up and blurted, "Where is your homo son and his husband?" – thinking he was being funny.

The customer, a typically gentle man, told me he threatened the owner that night. "If you ever call my son a 'homo' again," he said, "I will kill you." Neither he nor any member of his family ever returned. In that moment, a loyal customer chose his gay son's dignity over a favorite restaurant. It was the kind of allyship I wished I'd seen more of in my early days in the industry.

I think about that father's reaction often. It reminds me of my own father's restaurant, where I first learned to make quiche, where being different wasn't just tolerated but celebrated. I think about how far we've come and how far we still have to go. The phrase "real men don't eat quiche" seems almost quaint now, but its spirit lives on in a thousand different ways, in a thousand different kitchens and workplaces.

What I've learned through all of this is that being "fancy" — being true to who you are — isn't just a personal choice. It's a political act. Every quiche I made perfectly, every table I set beautifully, every kitchen I ran fairly was a kind of resistance. When people would ask me, "Why make it fancy?" what they were really asking was, "Why be yourself?" The answer, I finally understood, was simple: because anything else would be a lie.

Today, when I cook professionally or entertain at home, I make everything as fancy as I want. Every perfectly plated dish, every thoughtfully garnished plate, every beautifully set table is a statement: this is who I am, this is what I create, this is how I show love. Real men don't eat quiche? Well, this real man makes it, serves it, and celebrates it — along with everything else that makes him uniquely, unapologetically himself.

Because in the end, it was never really about the quiche. It was about the right to be yourself in a world that often demands conformity. It was about finding the courage to create beauty even when others mock it, about building spaces where everyone can bring their full selves to the table. Sometimes the most revolutionary act is simply being who you are, creating what you love, and serving it with pride.

A New Wave, Casserole Outing

I went to public school in Middle Tennessee during my high school years, riding the bus down from our mountain home in Sewanee to the valley below. The school's mascot was General Lee, Confederate flags were part of the official insignia, proudly displayed on team spirit posters, at pep rallies, and in our yearbooks. Our team name was the Rebels — as in "the South will rise again" Rebels. Even then, I understood the weight of these symbols, though I couldn't have articulated exactly why they made me feel so uneasy.

Every day on the bus, I sat with my friend Pam. We were united in our love of British new wave pop bands — Duran Duran, Wham!, Bananarama, Culture Club, and the like. We'd trade our Sony Walkman headsets back and forth, sharing our newest favorite cassettes we'd either bought or recorded from the radio. Our music was our armor, our way of creating a world beyond the confines of our rural Southern high school.

We styled ourselves to match our musical tastes — asymmetrical haircuts moussed with spiked tips, zipper-clad jackets adorned with band buttons and safety pins. We'd roll our acid-washed jeans up just above our scrunched-up socks, sometimes daring to wear neon sweatshirts purposely tattered with holes and worn off the shoulder. We were so proud of our sophisticated, big city looks. But in that rural area of Tennessee in the early 1980s, our fashion choices made us targets.

Most of our classmates hadn't caught up to our fashion sense — we were trying to be ahead of our time, and we paid the price for it. Although there was a large Black population at our school — many of them at the top of their class and members of the elected student body — not everyone was happy that Pam and I were besties. Pam was Black, and I was a sissy white boy, and our friendship seemed to offend certain people on a fundamental level.

For several months, a gang of farm boys in their cowboy hats and boots would wait to harass us as we entered the building together. They would call us unspeakable things — "N-word lover" and "faggot" — their words cutting through the morning air like knives. It didn't matter how many times we ignored them; like clockwork, they were always there to greet us with their laughter and taunts. It was intimidating, but we tried to forget about it and move on with our lives. We had each other, we had our music, we had our style. Sometimes that felt like enough. Sometimes it didn't.

Then came the semester when my homeroom study break was assigned to the vocational building — a separate wing of the school devoted to preparing students for immediate work after graduation. There were classes like wood shop, mechanics, welding, building, and farming. These were, and are, valuable programs, especially for rural areas where not all students were planning on college. There were also classes geared toward mostly young women at the time — beautician school and home economics. The gender division seems terribly outdated now, but that was how things were structured then.

This wasn't my favorite placement since the vocational wing was separate from the general part of school where academia and college prep were the mission. This particular wing was more oriented to the farm boys — the big lug types, with their country accents and conservative opinions — that I feared and attempted to avoid. I remember the first time I entered that home room. I was late because I had trouble finding it, and as I opened the door, the room went silent All of my daily tormentors turned around in their seats.

Then came the jeers, the derogatory words, the mocking noises. Someone knocked my books from my hands, and I scrambled to pick them up while every person in the classroom laughed. The teacher never stopped them. From that day forward, I sat in the back of the class so I could see everyone, my back against the wall in more ways than one. The teacher often left the room for most of the period. I just stuck quietly to my books and attempted to avoid any confrontation. They mostly ignored me, but not on one particular day.

This day I noticed something different. Some of them had brought little clubs and nunchucks; there was a stir of whispered conversation, an electric current of anticipation in the air. The teacher, once again, was nowhere to be found. One of the larger guys approached my desk, looming over me. "What's the matter with you, you little sissy boy?" he sneered.

At his words, more boys got up from their seats. Looking back now, I recognize that moment for what it was — the prelude to a hate crime, though we didn't have that term then. Thank goodness I was in the back of the class, in the seat closest to the door. I looked up at the boy right in front of me, at the boys gathering behind him with their clubs in hand, and made a split-second decision to protect myself. I ran.

Into the parking lot, heart pounding, feet barely touching the ground. Behind me, I could hear them — a pack of about twelve boys running after me, wielding their clubs and sticks like an angry mob going after Frankenstein's monster. Through the maze of cars I ran, finally diving under one of them. I tried not to breathe as I watched their feet shuffling by on the pavement, listening to their angry mutters and calls. "Where'd that faggot go?"

The minutes stretched like hours as I lay there, pressed against the cold ground, praying they wouldn't find me. When the bell finally rang, I waited until I was sure they were gone, then snuck back into the other wing of the building. I went straight to my art teacher's room, the one place I felt safe. In a panic and crying, I told her what had happened. She took me to the principal's office.

I remember nothing much was really done. I was moved to another homeroom, but I know those boys suffered little, if any, consequences. It wasn't until years later that I realized I had been gay bashed that day in homeroom, that I was victimized for just being. Those terms hadn't really taken hold in law and society yet.

Sometimes I still wonder: What if they had found me that day? How far would they have gone with their attack? That moment of terror has resurfaced quite a bit lately with the current political climate. It seems these issues have an ebb and flow to them. Sadly, I wasn't the last queer kid to be harassed, and it continues today.

But there was another space where I found safety, where I could be myself without fear — the kitchen. During this same period, something else was happening that would prove significant in ways I couldn't have imagined then. It started with a late-night conversation I overheard, one that seemed to confirm all my fears about being discovered, but would eventually help me understand who I really was.

One weekend during this terrifying period, my grandfather — "Tom Daddy," whom I adored — came up from Atlanta to visit us in the mountains. He was an amazing, open-minded man, especially for that time. This was 20 or so years before the gay community started to become accepted by mainstream American culture. Tom Daddy lived in Colony Square, a condominium that is now legendary for having had a large population of gay male tenants during the '70s and '80s, and even to this day.

We used to visit him often, and I can't even begin to explain the marvel of that modern mid-level high rise smack in the heart of Midtown Atlanta. It was the first of its kind back then. The "live-work-play" concept — as we call it today — was revolutionary. I remember it even had an ice-skating rink in the first level atrium. Now, as an openly gay man living in Atlanta myself, I understand better what that building represented — a safe haven, a community, a place where different ways of being were welcome. Where people could belong.

One night during his visit, after I was sent to bed, I listened in on his conversation with my father from my loft bedroom above the kitchen. Their talks usually became more adult-themed after I left, which of course made them irresistible to my young ears. My grandfather was explaining to my father that there were a lot of gay men living in his building. By the tone of his voice, I could tell this seemed quite normal to him, but also exceptional and cultural in a modern city way.

At this mention of gay men, my ears definitely perked up. He went on to explain that many of the people who worked and ran the restaurants on the first two levels of his condominium were also gay men. To me, the mere suggestion that gay men were noticeably gay, maybe even openly so, and that it was somehow normal was a foreign idea — but one that filled me with both delight and terror.

As he continued, he talked about one of his favorite restaurants that made fancy casseroles as one of its specialties. Then came the moment that would haunt me for months. The conversation culminated in the declaration: "Homosexual men just love to make casseroles!" I sank under my covers, my heart pounding. *Oh no,* I thought to myself. *This meant I had been discovered!* I was outed by a casserole.

You see, around the time I was 12, I had started making casseroles for my family. I was already very interested in cooking at a young age and had been experimenting on my own for maybe a year or so by the time I found casseroles. To my young mind, casseroles seemed fancy. This was the late 70s, so they kind of were. I had been tweaking different types of casserole recipes and presenting them to my family on a pretty regular basis. I thought I might be famous for my Spinach Casserole one day. It's still my favorite.

Back to "my discovery," as I sat listening to this damning conversation, I could imagine my dad's gears turning and thinking, *of course they do ... have you seen my son?* As I continued listening, I sank lower and lower into my bed and lay awake thinking *can they please change the subject?* Would I ever be able to make a casserole again? Had they known all along? Was every casserole I'd proudly presented to my family actually just another form of accidentally prancing about, unaware of my culinary flamboyance?

It's funny to think of this now, imagining I had just been outed by my grandfather's casual observation about gay men and their casseroles. For months after that night, I stayed away from my beloved spinach casserole — letting the heat of this declaration die down, I guess. But eventually, it showed back up in my repertoire, and it only got better and better over the years.

Looking back on this now stirs so many emotions. It's easy to laugh about it today, but like so many experiences growing up queer, it was quietly traumatic at the time. Here I was, already labeled a sissy by my peers, already running from literal gay bashers at school, and now even my cooking betrayed me. I was already struggling with the constant fear of being discovered, and now it seemed even my casseroles were giving me away.

But somehow, I persevered. Maybe because in our kitchen, unlike at school, I felt safe. My parents had always encouraged my cooking, praised my creativity, eaten every experimental dish I put in front of them. Even when I was dodging bullies at school, I knew I could come home and lose myself in the careful layering of a casserole, in the quiet satisfaction of watching cheese bubble and brown in the oven.

Now I understand that those casseroles were more than just dinner — they were a form of resistance, a way of staying true to myself even when I was afraid. Every spinach casserole I made was an act of courage, even if I didn't know it then. Like so many queer people before and after me, I found ways to express myself through creativity, through nurturing, through making things beautiful even when beauty felt dangerous.

Here is the recipe for my infamous spinach casserole. This recipe is nothing serious — remember, I was only 12 years old when I created it. But that's precisely what makes it special. It came from a place of pure creative instinct, before I knew anything about professional cooking, before I understood that loving to cook might mark me as different, before I learned to fear being "too fancy." It taught me something important: sometimes the simplest acts of being yourself are the most powerful.

I still make this dish today when I want something with the comfort of homemade flavors but without any pretense. It's easy to prepare in a few minutes and throw in the oven for a reasonably short time. It's absolute perfection on a cold rainy day. It stands on its own, but it's also fantastic with a crusty piece of garlic bread and a big glass of red wine. You can totally snuggle up on the couch with this one. And don't you dare scoff at the can of cream of mushroom soup. It is a casserole after all — and being authentic means embracing all parts of who you are, even the parts that aren't officially chef-fancy.

Spinach Casserole

Ingredients:

1 package of flat egg noodles, cooked to al dente
1 cup of sour cream or plain yogurt
1 can of cream of mushroom soup
1 cup cottage cheese (or ricotta is even better)
1 cup of grated cheese (cheddar, jack, Colby or mozzarella)
¼ cup grated Parmesan
1 clove garlic minced

Fresh or dried chopped herbs (oregano, basil, sage and/or thyme)

1 tsp. salt

½ tsp. ground black pepper

6 saltine crackers (crushed in a baggie with a rolling pin)

2 tsp. Olive oil

½ tsp. paprika

¼ tsp. grated nutmeg

10 oz. pkg. Frozen chopped spinach (thawed and strained) or 1 16 oz. bag fresh spinach sautéed, strained and chopped

Directions:

Adjust oven rack to middle position and preheat to 350 degrees

Mix noodles, sour cream/yogurt, cream of mushroom, cottage cheese, grated cheese, Parmesan, garlic, herbs, salt and pepper in large bowl until well blended

Scoop mixture into greased casserole dish

Mix remaining ingredients with olive oil and top evenly to make a toasty crust

Place casserole on middle rack and bake for 40 minutes

Hint:

Place casserole on cookie sheet while cooking to catch any drippings.

Now, as I enjoy this casserole snuggled up with my cat, Bijou, I relive those moments of my grandfather's stories about city life in Atlanta during the early 1980s, and the day I discovered that being gay might be normal ... that gay men making casseroles was normal too. What once filled me with terror now fills me with pride. Each time I make this dish, I think about that scared boy in the loft, listening to conversations about gay men and their casseroles, and I wish I could tell him: "You're going to be okay. More than okay. Those things you're afraid mark you as different? They're going to become your superpowers. They're going to make you fancy."

The truth is, being "fancy" — whether it's in cooking, entertaining, decorating, or just moving through the world — isn't something to hide or apologize for. It's a gift. Every casserole I made, every table I set, every flower I arranged was teaching me how to be myself, even when I didn't realize it. Those creative acts were keeping me whole during times when the world seemed determined to break me.

Today, my cooking is as fancy as I want it to be. Sometimes that means elaborate French techniques I learned in professional kitchens. Sometimes it means a homey casserole that takes me back to my childhood kitchen. Both are equally valid, equally authentic expressions of who I am. Understanding this has freed me to create without fear, to nurture without apology, to be fancy in whatever way feels true to me in the moment.

Because here's what I finally learned: those boys in home room who tried to beat the fancy out of me? They failed. My creativity, my love of beauty, my desire to nurture through food — these weren't weaknesses to be ashamed of. They were strengths that would carry me through the darkest times and ultimately lead me to a life filled with purpose and joy.

That casserole-making boy in the loft grew up to be exactly who he was meant to be — a chef, an entertainer, a creator of beautiful experiences. And yes, he still makes a mean spinach casserole. Because real men do eat quiche, and gay men do make casseroles, and being yourself — completely, unapologetically yourself — is the fanciest thing of all.

The Women Who Saw Me

When I was around eleven, my dad took me out of school on a weekday in October, telling me he had an adventure planned. Just the two of us — no brothers, no responsibilities, just an open road and a promise of something special ahead. This was when he owned Shenanigans, the local eatery in our small university town of Sewanee, Tennessee. We were heading to Apalachicola, Florida on what he called a "shrimp run" — driving south to buy fresh shrimp and oysters directly from the fishermen for the restaurant.

But this journey would become about much more than seafood. Along the way, my father introduced me to three women who had shaped his life, and who would, in turn, help shape mine. Each of them, in their own way, would teach me something crucial about being true to myself in a world that often demanded conformity.

Our first stop was Daphne, Alabama, a small town on Mobile Bay where my dad grew up in the late 1940s and early 1950s. As we drove, he shared stories of his childhood in the Deep South — stories that revealed both the beauty and the pain of that time and place. He told me about segregated water fountains, about his grandmother throwing packs of cigarettes from her car to men working on chain gangs because she felt sorry for them. He spoke of his Black boyhood friends who lived down the dirt road, and how they were treated so differently from white boys like himself. He remembered getting in trouble for calling an adult Black male "Sir," and the nonsensical explanation he was given for why that was wrong.

Jackson Browne and Joni Mitchell played on the car stereo as we drove, their lyrics about love and justice and change floating through the warm Southern air. I still know every word to those songs, each one a reminder of that pivotal journey.

We visited his childhood home first — a big white two-story house on the bay in Daphne. Originally built by a French family as their summer home, it stood on raised foundations with screened porches lining the entire front facade and back. Floor-to-ceiling double-hung windows flanked all sides, and enormous trees draped with Spanish moss lined the front walkway. I could see the long dock behind the house stretching into the water, with a boathouse to the side and a cottage house in the back.

Joy lit up my father's face as he shared tales of growing up in that house with his sisters and parents. He told me how they would fish with a large net near their dock, a wide badminton-like net called a seine with sinkers on the bottom and floaties on top. They would drag it from the dock to the shore, catching pounds of shrimp and crab along with whatever else happened to get swept up in their harvest.

The house was called "Jubilee Lodge," named for a natural phenomenon unique to Mobile Bay where sea life would become stranded on the shore during certain low-tide conditions, allowing locals to gather seafood simply by picking it up from where it lay. This happens in only two places in the world, my father told me, and south Alabama was one of them. But the real jubilee — the true celebration — was still to come.

Before we get to that, let me share one of the very first things that struck me as "fancy," though it might be pretty common these days. To my young boy's eyes, it was the pinnacle of elegance, one originating from the sort of "shrimp run" I took with my dad: The simple (and fantastic) shrimp cocktail.

Classic Gulf Shrimp Cocktail

When I remember that day at the Apalachicola docks, watching weathered fishermen sort their fresh catch, I think about how far a shrimp travels from boat to cocktail glass. While we can't always get dock-fresh seafood, we can honor those fishermen by preparing shrimp with care and attention. This recipe elevates the standard shrimp cocktail with proper poaching technique and a homemade sauce that puts bottled versions to shame. Always serve with a sprig of parsley—it's not just garnish, it's tradition.

For the Shrimp:

2 pounds large shrimp (16/20 count), preferably Gulf shrimp

2 lemons, halved

1 yellow onion, quartered

4 cloves garlic, crushed

2 bay leaves

1 Tbsp. whole black peppercorns

¼ cup kosher salt

4 quarts water

Large bowl of ice water for shocking

For the Cocktail Sauce:

1 cup Heinz chili sauce (no substitutes)

¼ cup prepared horseradish (or more to taste)

2 Tbsp. fresh squeezed lemon juice

1 Tbsp. Worcestershire sauce

¼ tsp. Tabasco sauce

⅛ tsp. celery salt

For Serving:

Fresh parsley sprigs

Lemon wedges

Additional horseradish on the side

Martini glasses or small bowls for presentation

Directions:

Peel and de-vein shrimp, leaving tails on. Reserve shells.

In a large pot, combine water, reserved shells, lemon halves, onion, garlic, bay leaves, peppercorns, and salt.

Bring to a boil, reduce heat, and simmer 20 minutes to create flavorful broth.

Strain broth, return to pot, and bring back to a simmer.

Add shrimp and cook just until they turn pink and curl, about 3 minutes.

Immediately remove with slotted spoon and plunge into ice water.

Once cool, drain and pat dry.

For sauce, whisk all ingredients together in bowl. Adjust horseradish to taste.

Chill shrimp and sauce separately for at least 2 hours.

To serve, arrange shrimp around the rim of martini glass or small bowl.

Place sauce in center.

Garnish with parsley sprig and lemon wedge.

Serve additional horseradish on the side.

Notes on Presentation:

Arrange shrimp so tails point upward, creating height. If using martini glasses, a small piece of lettuce in the bottom helps anchor the sauce cup. Always provide a small empty dish for shells — it's these little touches that elevate the experience from cocktail hour to elegant entertaining.

After we left Jubilee Lodge, we stopped at a smaller house. It was yellow, with green and white metal awnings hanging over windows dressed in colorful flower boxes. My dad wasn't entirely sure if this was the right place, so he told me to wait in the car while he approached the door.

From the car, I watched as an elderly Black woman answered hesitantly, opening the storm door just a crack and asking, "Yes ... may I help you?"

My father must have been quite a sight — his longish red hair and beard giving him that "hippie look" that made some people nervous in the South. But then something magical happened. The woman's face transformed as recognition dawned. She threw the door wide open and her arms even wider, embracing my father as she repeated, "My precious memory, my precious memory," joyful tears streaming down her face.

This was Miss Lilian Varlee, the woman my father lovingly called his "second mother," and watching their reunion, I understood why. She had been his caregiver when he was a boy, though that clinical term doesn't begin to capture what she meant to him. From the stories he'd told me in the car, she was the one who had taught him that love doesn't conform to society's rules, that care transcends color lines, that family isn't just about blood.

My father waved for me to come up onto the porch, and Miss Lilian invited us into her home. "This is Miss Lilian," my dad said simply, but his voice carried the weight of history, of love, of complicated Southern relationships that a child like me was just beginning to understand. I had only known of her from my father's stories until this trip, but I would come to understand more about their relationship as I grew older, reading books and watching films about the Old South. Their bond represented something both beautiful and painful about our region's history — the deep connections formed across racial lines, even in a time of formal separation.

Miss Lilian's home was a wonderland to my young eyes. Every surface held treasures — it was packed with bric-a-brac and knickknacks that I couldn't help but touch, though I was gently reminded not to. I was particularly fascinated by a big bowl of acrylic grapes in all colors — the kind I now see in antique stores and that my friends collect. Seeing them always takes me back to that day, to the warmth of Miss Lilian's home and the love that filled it.

As they caught up, I sipped from the ice-cold bottle of Coca-Cola Miss Lilian had given me and took in every detail of her magical home. It was more than just a house — it was a lesson in how to make a space truly your own, how to fill it with things that bring you joy, how to create beauty even in modest circumstances. Looking back now, I realize her home influenced my decorative taste in ways I'm still discovering. It was warm, inviting, and absolutely authentic — like Miss Lilian herself.

There was both joy and melancholy in that visit — something my young self sensed but couldn't quite name. Here was this woman who had shaped my father's heart, who had loved him as her "precious memory" through years when such love had to be carefully navigated. I felt instantly connected to her, recognizing perhaps that she too understood what it meant to love differently, to care deeply in ways society didn't always validate.

That was regrettably the only day I would spend with Miss Lilian, but its impact rippled through my life in unexpected ways. Her home taught me that beauty doesn't need to follow rules — that a bowl of plastic grapes could be art if arranged with love, that a modest yellow house could hold more magic than a mansion. She showed me that creating your own space, filling it with things that speak to your heart, is a form of courage.

Years later, when friends tease me about my "old lady chic" decorating style, I think of Miss Lilian's house. I think of how she made that space completely her own, how every trinket and treasure told a story, how she created beauty without apology. In my own way, I've tried to do the same — to make spaces that reflect who I really am, not who others think I should be.

But Miss Lilian wasn't the only woman who would teach me about being true to myself.

Back home in Tennessee, I found another sanctuary in my father's restaurant kitchen, where Alice, our main chef, became my after-school confidante. Every afternoon, I'd walk to the restaurant from my school bus stop, and in that kitchen, I found something precious: acceptance.

Alice was always there, ready to listen to my stories, to really hear what I was going through. She got to know my struggles better than almost anyone else during those teenage years. In her kitchen, I could be myself without fear or pretense. She recognized my creative spirit and forgave what others saw as shortcomings. She helped me see that being different wasn't a flaw — it was a gift.

We would drink hot apple cider together as we talked, and I would make myself big cheesy sandwiches and eat pretzels. Often, she'd serve me a bowl of her homemade soup or a slice of quiche. But more nourishing than any food was her steady presence, her quiet validation of who I was becoming. She would share stories from her own teen years, helping me understand that the pain of being different eventually gives way to something beautiful — if you're brave enough to stay true to yourself.

But it was Karen Mauze who would change everything. She was different from the other adults in my parents' social circle — she saw me with a clarity that was both thrilling and terrifying. At potlucks and gatherings, while other grown-ups talked over my head, Karen would get down to my level, really talk to me, really listen. She would tell me stories and jokes, but more importantly, she acknowledged the struggle I was trying so hard to hide.

Karen recognized my battle with traditional boy roles and did something revolutionary: she told me it was okay. Not just okay — she helped me understand that my differences could be strengths. She taught me about great male ballet dancers and renowned chefs. She showed me how girls could build houses, play sports, and grow up to be senators. It wasn't just talk — she backed it up with action.

One day, Karen mentioned she was taking ballet classes and asked if I would want to try the children's classes at the same studio. I shyly agreed, though inside my heart was racing with excitement.

At the next potluck, to my amazement, she brought me a paper bag containing black tights and black ballet slippers. Without my knowledge, she had talked to my parents, and they had all agreed that she could sign me up for children's dance classes at the university. She would even take me to and from my classes.

I remember opening that paper bag in front of the partygoers and feeling simultaneously uneasy and thrilled. It was as if there was a secret in that bag that no one should know, yet here was an adult not only acknowledging it but celebrating it. I could hardly wait to get home and try everything on. Finally, in the semi-privacy of our only bathroom, I pulled on the tights — at first backwards, then figured out the right way. When they were properly on, with all the kinks pulled out and no twisted areas, *they felt amazing!* I quickly put on the shoes and the plain white t-shirt that was also in the bag and looked in the mirror. *I looked amazing!*

I felt something entirely new, almost titillating, if that's possible at seven. Something that felt like freedom, like permission to be fully myself. I danced around and made gestures that looked like ballet to me. The sensation was so new and liberating. I felt like me, and for once, that feeling was allowed. I mean, I was actually going to be able to wear this in public — at least during my lessons.

The reality of ballet class was both more wonderful and more complicated than my bathroom mirror dancing had prepared me for. When I went to my first class, I was the only boy among about fifteen children. Many of the girls were my peers from grade school, and even my cousin Maggie was there. The floors were laminated wood gym floors that creaked when you walked across them — but in a good way, a way that made everything feel official and important. One wall had bars at adult waist level for holding while practicing, and across from that was an entire wall of mirrors. A piano and bench sat in the corner, with one metal folding chair toward the center.

I sat on the floor with the other girls that first day as we waited for the teacher, my heart pounding. Some of them looked at me funny and asked why I was there. Some even told me flat out that ballet was for girls. I felt the familiar shame creeping in, but then I remembered what Karen had told me. I thought about those great male ballet dancers she'd mentioned, about how some football players took ballet to build agility and stamina. Karen had armed me with facts to defend my right to be there.

Then the door opened, and a handsome, lanky man with dark hair walked in. He must have been in his mid-to-late 20s, and to my amazement, he announced himself as our instructor. I couldn't help giving the other girls a proud look, as if to silently say, "See, I told you ballet was for boys too." He was a lovely man with an elegant manner, and he did something I'll never forget: he took special time with me after showing the girls their moves, carefully instructing me in the male counterpart's traditional steps.

It was an amazing, eye-opening time in my early childhood. For the first time, I felt proud to be myself, and I was being backed up by both adults and children alike. This instructor made me feel normal — more than normal, he made me feel special. He showed me that being different could be an advantage, not a flaw.

But then, only a month into my classes, something happened that would haunt me for years. When I showed up for class one day, our regular instructor wasn't there; a woman was there in his place. She told us she was to be our new instructor. I had so many questions, but somehow I knew they shouldn't be asked.

Where was he? Why didn't he say goodbye? Who was this new teacher?

Everyone else just went along with it as if it were normal. Sadly, the new teacher didn't take time to show me the separate traditional male steps and positions. I remember feeling lost and forgotten, made to do the same steps as the girls. The memories grow foggy after that, but I know I lost interest and didn't continue to the next level of classes. I've always regretted not going back.

It wasn't until years later, in my mid-teens, that I learned our instructor was gay and had likely died by suicide. Learning this was overwhelming, considering I was just discovering my own sexuality. Was I ...? Surely not. It was just a phase, right? The weight of this realization wouldn't fully hit me until a therapy session in my late 30s, when my therapist helped me understand that this early loss — of both a role model and a safe space — had shaped me more than I knew.

But through all of this, there was Karen. After each ballet class, successful or struggling, she would take me for yogurt and a sandwich. We'd sit on a bench together, and she'd listen as I processed everything I was feeling, though I couldn't always find the words. Yogurt was trendy then, and eating it made me feel sophisticated and cultured — no pun intended. Just like wheat germ and bean sprouts, avocados and granola were becoming popular, there was a sense that new things were possible, that old boundaries were breaking down.

Karen understood something crucial that I'm only now fully appreciating: she knew that every child needs champions — adults who see them fully and love them just as they are. She didn't just support my interest in ballet; she actively created space for it to flourish. She didn't just tell me it was okay to be different; she showed me how difference could be beautiful. She gently nodded to my still-hidden fancy. She acknowledged it was there, even before I knew it was.

I think it took courage for her to give me courage. In that time and place, encouraging a boy to take ballet wasn't a small thing. She risked judgment from others to help me face my own fears. She and my ballet instructor helped me feel normal, helped those girls in class see that I was one of them. That ballet isn't just for girls. That art and beauty belong to everyone.

Today, when I set a beautiful table or plate a perfect dish, when I arrange flowers or design a space, I think of Karen. I think of how she taught me that there were great male artists of all kinds, that gender shouldn't limit anyone's expression. I thank my parents for allowing Karen's encouragement, for understanding that their son needed this kind of support and validation.

The yogurt and talks with Karen were about more than just after-class refreshment — they were about creating a space where I could be fully myself, where my interests and inclinations weren't just tolerated but celebrated. She showed me that being fancy wasn't a flaw but a gift, that my creativity wasn't something to hide but something to nurture.

Looking back now, I see how fortunate I was to have these three women in my life, each showing me a different facet of what it meant to be authentically myself in a world that often demanded conformity. Miss Lilian, who created beauty and love in a time and place that tried to deny both to her. Alice, who made her kitchen a sanctuary where a confused teenager could find acceptance and understanding. And Karen, who not only saw who I really was but actively helped me become that person.

They formed a kind of loving trinity of acceptance, each offering their own form of grace. Miss Lilian showed me that you could create beauty anywhere, that a modest house could become a treasure box of self-expression if you were brave enough to make it so. Her home taught me that what others might dismiss as "too much" or "old lady chic" could actually be perfect if it truly reflected who you were.

Alice's kitchen wisdom went far beyond recipes. She taught me that nurturing others through food was a form of love that transcended gender expectations. In her kitchen, there was no such thing as "women's work" or "men's work" — there was just the work of creating something beautiful and nourishing. Her quiet acceptance gave me space to develop my own culinary voice, to trust my instincts about both food and life.

And Karen — my dear, good Karen — she did more than just give me permission to dance. She showed me that being different wasn't something to survive but something to celebrate. Those after-ballet talks over yogurt were really lessons in self-acceptance, in finding the courage to be fancy in a world that often preferred the bland.

What's crucial here is to recognize the importance adult role models play in children's lives. I will never forget what these women did for me. Their influence lives on in every beautifully set table, every carefully crafted dish, every moment when I choose to express rather than suppress my creative spirit. They taught me that the very things that made me different — my attention to detail, my love of beauty, my desire to nurture — were actually my greatest strengths.

To any child struggling to be themselves, to any adult wondering how to help such a child, I offer this wisdom learned from these three remarkable women: Create safe spaces where authenticity can flourish. Show children that their differences are gifts, not flaws. Help them understand they're not alone, that there's a whole world of people who will eventually see and celebrate their unique beauty.

Most importantly, be like Karen — brave enough to give others courage. Be like Alice — willing to offer sanctuary when the world feels hostile. Be like Miss Lilian — determined to create beauty even in challenging circumstances. Because sometimes the greatest act of resistance is simply being yourself, and helping others do the same.

These women taught me that there are many ways to be strong, many ways to be brave, many ways to be beautiful. Their lessons live on in every casserole I proudly serve, every ballet performance I attend, every space I dare to make fancy. They showed me that authenticity is the greatest art of all, and that living truthfully is the most beautiful dance we can perform.

The Beauty of Being Too Much

Since I was a young boy, even as young as four years old, I've been a smeller of roses, a flower-picker, and sometimes — I must confess — a sneaky flower picker at that. My earliest memories are perfumed with blooms: hazy, dreamlike flashbacks of making daisy chains in grassy fields on warm summer days. I remember hiking through Abbo's Alley, a nature reserve in my hometown of Sewanee, Tennessee during the early spring months, my heart racing at the sight of thousands of blooming bulbs — daffodils, buttercups, paper whites, hyacinths; all colors and shapes of tulips, irises, and crocuses. The indigenous redbuds, wild azaleas, dogwoods, Japanese magnolias, and forsythia burst into bloom every year like nature's own coming-out party.

The smell of wild honeysuckle and primrose every May in the South still takes me back to those days, to the end of the school year and the blessed beginning of three months' summer break. The Tennessee roadsides of my youth overflowed with Queen Anne's lace, Shasta daisies, wild clover, baby aster, thistle, and countless others. Walking the trails in the woods around our early home, usually with my father, we would discover fairy-like woodland wildflowers with magical names: pipsissewa, trillium, wild bluebells, fire pinks, Jack in the pulpit, and the ever-elusive lady slipper orchid. There were ferns of every variety, mountain laurel, wild sorrel and sassafras — so many types I couldn't begin to name them all, though I tried to learn every single one.

I loved the flowers that mom grew in the garden too — nasturtium, zinnias, marigolds, snowball viburnum, four o'clocks, peonies, lilacs, and agapanthus. Each one was a different kind of beautiful, each one teaching me that nature offered endless variations on perfection.

Whether they came from my mom's carefully tended beds, woodland paths, or the side of the road, I was drawn to them with an intensity I couldn't explain and, for years, didn't dare to fully understand.

I would bring them home proudly but carefully, arranging them in Mason jars and vases with the same attention to detail that professional florists might use. I'd set them in the center of the dining table or in a kitchen windowsill and admire them until they faded. Each arrangement was a small act of creation, a way of bringing beauty into our daily lives. I loved learning about them too — not just their names but their seasons, their habits, what made each one unique.

My dad would teach me the name of every wildflower and plant on our hikes around our house, while my mom would teach me about the horticultural side — how to plant, when to harvest, which flowers worked best in arrangements. When I learned about flowers in my seventh-grade science class, I would search for the perfect daffodil specimens to dissect. I would carefully separate the different parts of the flowers, pin them on a board and label them, fascinated by how something so beautiful could also be so precisely structured.

But here's my confession, one that still makes me smile: I didn't just pick flowers from my mom's garden and along the sides of roads and trails. I also loved snagging them sneakily from neighbors' yards and public parks. And I have never outgrown this favorite pastime of mine. In fact, I was recently caught picking magnolias from the trees — and subsequently scolded by the groundskeeper — at the Jimmy Carter Library Garden grounds near my home in Atlanta.

In my defense, however, I've always picked flowers under the assumption that I knew what I was doing. I did not, and would not, pick someone's prize-winning, front-of-the-row peony, and I never picked more than my share. I gingerly pick them in a pruning-like manner, "as to promote new growth," *your honor.* At least that's what I tell myself. And of course, I make sure they are flowers from the back side of the bed or ones that cannot be seen well by the general public. Besides, I pay my taxes, right? For this reason, a couple of my good friends refer to me as "the Flower Bandit."

However, no matter how pretty, creative, or festive my arrangements have been, as a child I always felt some sense of shame regarding my love of flowers and decorating. This shame wasn't about my minor crimes as the Flower Bandit — it was about my love of flowers in the first place. Especially as a child, picking flowers from the side of the road in my hometown neighborhood, I felt ashamed because it was looked down upon for a boy to pick flowers. I was labeled a sissy for liking nature. Had I loved the woods — *fine.* But flowers? That was too much.

I should note — and this matters deeply — it was never my parents who made me feel ashamed of my flower collecting. In fact, they encouraged me, telling me how beautiful my arrangements were, praising my eye for color and composition. The shame came from that general sense bestowed by society, that invisible but crushing weight that said boys shouldn't love beautiful things, shouldn't want to create beauty, shouldn't be *fancy.*

How could loving such beautiful things, these amazing gifts of nature, be wrong? How could arranging them into festive centerpieces for others to enjoy be somehow against the rules of society? I have never understood this thinking, though I felt its effects deeply. It was this way with so many things I loved as a boy — flower arranging, cooking, gardening, ballet. Each passion came with its own burden of shame, its own need for secrecy.

So I developed strategies. I'd hide my flowers behind my back when cars or dog walkers passed during my picking excursions. I'd hurry my prized finds home as quickly as possible, as if smuggling contraband. *Nothing to see here. Carry on,* I would think to myself. *No sissies here.* But once safely inside, I would lose myself in the pure joy of creation, in the careful balancing of colors and heights, in the search for perfect containers to showcase nature's gifts.

Today, I worry much less when I'm "flower banditting" about. But I still feel it ... that old anxiety can surface when I'm thinking of plucking a few stems along my paths. That childhood guilt bubbles up and has to be pushed back down with a good talking to myself. Yet here's what's remarkable: it never stopped me. Not when I was young, not now. Something in me knew that this love of beauty was too essential to who I was to be denied.

I can say now that my family's acceptance, including my brothers', was the encouragement I deserved and desperately needed. Today, I always have flowers or fresh cut greenery of some sort in my home. Even as I write, I'm enjoying some beautiful daffodils in a vase on my table, their sunny faces reminding me of all the beauty I nearly denied myself out of fear.

I should have never been made to feel embarrassed for enjoying what I loved. Little boys should never be made to feel less for picking flowers, or for wanting to dance, or being "fancy." Of course, the same goes for all children, no matter their gender, sexuality, or what brings them joy. I will always pick flowers. I will always arrange them on tables sparkling with china and lapped in linen. And I will admire them over a beautiful meal as I visit with my dear family or friends as long as I am able.

This embrace of beauty, this refusal to tone myself down, eventually found its way into every corner of my life. Another love of mine became finding old treasures for my home. I don't think there could ever be too much — and that phrase, "too much," would become something of a personal revolution. Ever since I can remember, I've been drawn to old homes and the treasures that filled them. Any chance to explore an antique shop filled to the brim with heirlooms and rare oddities would set my heart racing. An antique store isn't just a shop to me — it's a museum of what once was, and a laboratory for what might be.

I grew up around homes that showed me different ways of creating beauty. There was my "Mama-ma" Sprunk on my mom's side, with her state-of-the-art, midcentury-modern-slash-nouveau-riche style — all clean lines and bold statements. Then there was Grandmama Brown, my dad's mother, with her classic Victorian eclecticism mixed with ancient Asian arts collections. Every visit to her home was like traveling through time and across continents.

My Aunt Margie created her own beautiful Florida room style, adorned with enormous houseplants, chandeliers, and beautiful paintings — a perfect blend of natural and crafted beauty. And my Aunt Lee developed her unique take on Victorian meets rural buff side woodland living, proving that elegance could exist anywhere. Even that one precious day I spent in Miss Lilian's home showed me how beauty could transcend circumstances, how a modest house could become a treasure box of memories and meaning.

Each of these women crafted spaces that were completely, unabashedly themselves. They taught me that decorating isn't about following rules or trends — it's about creating a space that tells your story. Over the years, I've developed my own eclectic style, but one that was influenced by all these great ladies of my life. I never pass up the opportunity to receive an heirloom from the family — dinner tablewares, knick-knacks, or furniture. Just the other day, I acquired a stunning collection of Waterford cordials that were originally my Grandmama Brown's. When my cousin Rachel said she didn't use them enough and was sure that I would, she was absolutely right. They look wonderful with a perfect ice-cold pour of Green Chartreuse.

I use my old china sets and serving pieces as often as possible. I particularly adore pieces that were made for highly specific purposes — the kind of items that some might call fussy or unnecessary, but that I see as celebrations of life's little ceremonies. Take, for example, when my Aunt Margie recently asked if I wanted the set of pot de crème pots my Grandmama Brown had bequeathed to her. I thought to myself, *is she nuts?* Who does she think she's talking to? Of course I wanted them.

She was definitely talking to the right person, and I have gladly added them to my collection. The following Easter, my good friend Michael filled them with the most delightfully rich chocolate custard and cream for the annual Easter supper I host. Each one of the set of ten is about three ounces, made of white ribbed fluted porcelain with delicately twisted grape leaf and vine-like handles and lids. They're exactly the kind of "unnecessary" items that make life beautiful.

How my friends and I revel in the magic of those little pots! There's actually a set of tiny, accompanying pot de crème spoons that my aunt forgot to bring with her when I was given the pots. I make it my duty to remind her every time we talk, not to forget to bring them on her next visit. We haven't seen her for two years, but she's packed them and is bringing them with her when she visits next. Of course, I can't wait to see her first and foremost after all this time, but I also can barely wait to see those little pots and spoons reunited.

Yes, I have china cabinets and closets arranged with these collections, but they don't sit there getting dusty. I've never understood why people waste their heirlooms in dark cabinets. This is our chance to use them. Yes, they might get broken or chipped, but that's okay — better to be broken in service of joy than to sit pristine and unused. These beautiful pieces were meant to be seen, to be part of life's daily celebrations.

I do have modern pieces too, but I've learned over the years that eclecticism — mixing both old and new pieces from different time periods and aesthetics — is what really makes a home. I confess, however, that I am a maximalist, and this isn't for everyone. But even minimalists should mix in old pieces. A house full of ultra-modern will become a house full of ultra-dated really quick. For this reason, most of my closest friends have lovingly labeled my style as "old lady chic," and it is a title I'm most proud to hold. Apologies to my living aunts — it's not my fault. They said it, not me. Heavy is the head that wears this queen's crown.

Though this might not be your style, and maybe you don't want to spend the rest of your life dusting, I encourage everyone to have some eclectic moments in their home. If your family isn't handing things down to you, then find some treasures for yourself. Antique stores and even thrift stores are filled with diamonds in the rough, just waiting to be loved and brought back to life. Think of it as recycling — we should use what we already have, no reason to buy something new and trendy that will become passé.

There's a powerful irony in how my childhood love of flowers, once something I had to hide, has bloomed into this unabashed celebration of beauty in all its forms. That little boy who once hid flowers behind his back now fills his home with more beauty than some might think necessary — and that's exactly the point. Because what I've learned is that "too much" is often just enough when it comes to expressing who you really are.

Every time I set a table with multiple patterns of china, layer linens of different textures, or mix crystal and pottery on the same surface, I'm doing more than decorating — I'm making a statement about abundance, about joy, about the right to take up space in the world. Each time I rescue some "old lady" item from a thrift store or gratefully receive another family heirloom, I'm not just collecting things — I'm collecting possibilities for beauty, for connection, for celebration.

Being fancy isn't about money or status — it's about attention, care, and the courage to express joy. It's about understanding that a dinner party served on mixed-matched plates can be more beautiful than one with a perfect set of expensive china. It's about knowing that those pot de crème pots aren't just serving pieces — they're vessels for memories, for stories, for love.

I've come to understand that my early fascination with flowers, my love of beautiful objects, my desire to create special moments weren't signs of being "too much" — they were early expressions of who I was meant to be. That boy who once carefully arranged wildflowers in Mason jars grew up to create spaces where beauty isn't just allowed, it's celebrated. Where "fancy" isn't a criticism, but a compliment of the highest order.

And by all means, if you're offered some ancient or not-so-ancient item you don't want, don't throw it away. Give it to another maximalist in your life, or to me. Someone else will find an ingenious way to use it, to find the beauty in it. Because that's what being fancy really means — seeing the potential for beauty everywhere, creating moments of joy from whatever's at hand, and sharing that joy with others.

The Flower Bandit grew up to be exactly who he was meant to be — someone who makes the world a little more beautiful, a little more fancy, one borrowed bloom, one rescued treasure, one carefully set table at a time. And if that's too much? Well, too much is exactly enough when it comes to living life fully, authentically, and fabulously.

Because in the end, fancy isn't just about aesthetics — it's about courage. The courage to love what you love, to create what you create, to be who you are without apology. It's about transforming shame into celebration, hiding into displaying, fear into fierce joy. So go ahead — be too much. Set that elaborate table. Mix those patterns. Save those old serving pieces. Pick those flowers (carefully, of course). Make life as fancy as you dare. After all, if being fancy is wrong, I don't want to be right.

The Art of Creating Grace

I've worked in restaurants — and I can hardly believe I'm saying this — for over 30 years. In that time, I've learned that how people treat servers, bartenders, and kitchen staff reveals more about them than any resume or social media profile ever could. I've seen the best and worst of human nature play out over plates of food, and I've come to understand that creating beauty isn't just about what's on the plate — it's about how we treat each other in the process.

90 percent of the clientele I've served throughout my career have been good customers. Out of that 90 percent, 5 percent have been incredible — the kind of people who make you remember why you fell in love with hospitality in the first place. These were the ones I couldn't wait to see walk in the door, who treated me as an equal or even looked up to me for my talents. They were the ones who would share beautiful dusty bottles of aged French wine from their cellars, who sent genuine compliments to the kitchen, who understood that generosity isn't just about the size of the tip (though their 50 percent gratuities didn't hurt).

These special customers were the ones I made sure to visit at their tables, listening to stories about their travels or recipes they'd been trying at home. They understood when things were hectic and remained patient when errors occurred. These kinds of customers hardly ever complained, but if they did, they did it with respect to the staff and to me. Their feedback was always offered as collaboration, not criticism.

A lot of times, honest feedback from these gracious customers was exactly what I needed to hear to make things better. They understood something fundamental: that being fancy isn't just about what you wear or how you set a table — it's about maintaining your sparkle even when things get difficult. These customers got treated well not because they demanded it, but because they radiated the kind of grace that makes others want to rise to their level.

Trust me, these customers get the best of everything — not because they insist on it, but because they inspire it. They always get the best seats, their special requests are happily met, their preferences remembered. And here's the magic: when I get to send these sweetest of customers free appetizers and desserts, or a round of drinks, they receive these gifts with the same grace they show others. Sometimes they buy me a drink in return, or bring me fresh-baked cookies, or remember me with a holiday gift. It's not about the exchange of things — it's about the exchange of dignity.

Then there's that other 10 percent — the ones who seem to check their humanity at the door. The kind of person who degrades the host or gets touchy-feely with servers. Clients who arrive angry, their fury having nothing to do with us but everything to do with how they view service workers. There are regulars (unfortunately) you can smell coming a mile away, with their high-maintenance attitude and a chip on their shoulder the size of Mount Rushmore.

Sometimes, I feel some of them simply get treated badly at their own jobs or elsewhere, and they take this chance to have a little bit of power and abuse it to the nth degree. I've definitely had my share of talking crying servers down from walking out the back door due to abusive behavior from a customer. These moments taught me something crucial about being fancy: true elegance isn't about putting others down to lift yourself up. It's about maintaining your shine while helping others find theirs.

It's easy to abuse power in the restaurant business because we always have to bend over backwards to please the customer. You can act like a complete fool, and we still have to smile and try to correct any problems you might have, though non-medical assistance can only go so far with some customers. But here's what these difficult customers never understand: when you dim someone else's light, you don't make your own shine brighter.

Both the front- and back-of-house staff have more integrity than most difficult customers might imagine. While they might assume we're retaliating behind the scenes — spitting in food or dropping things on the floor — that's not how we operate. In my 30 years, I've seen maybe one or two incidents of such unacceptable behavior, which was always dealt with immediately. Our approach is actually far more elegant: we simply give our best to those who know how to receive it gracefully.

It's actually the opposite of what these demanding customers might expect. We treat those who show respect with extra care, extra attention, extra flourishes that transform a meal into an experience. In fact, due to my long experience in the business and my ultimate empathy, I go out of my way to be that best customer when I dine out now.

I'm always patient. I never send back food without a genuinely good reason. I'm never overly demanding. And yes, I always over-tip. What happens when I go out? I get fit in on a busy night at the last minute. I always get the best seat if it's available. I often get surprise appetizers from the chef. The staff is genuinely excited to see me when I walk in the door. Basically, I get treated like gold. Trust me, servers and bartenders remember how well or how badly you tip, but more importantly, they remember how you made them feel.

The moral of the story is simple: "Don't be an asshole." Not in a restaurant or anywhere else for that matter. But it goes deeper than that — being fancy isn't just about knowing which fork to use or how to properly hold a wine glass. It's about understanding that true elegance comes from how you treat people, especially those in service positions. You want to go where everybody knows your name? Then get to know them and treat them well. It will come back to you. It is the purest form of instant karma.

I've come to understand that being fancy isn't just an aesthetic — it's an ethic. It's about maintaining your sparkle when your soup is cold, when your reservation is lost, when the kitchen is backed up. It's about understanding that the person serving you is someone's child, someone's parent, someone's whole world.

Real sophistication — real fanciness — works in the opposite direction. It lifts people up. It creates moments of beauty even in difficult situations. It transforms ordinary interactions into opportunities for grace.

I think about the regular customers who became like family over the years. There was an elderly woman who always ordered the same thing — a simple chicken dish — but made everyone feel like they were serving her at a royal banquet. She'd ask about the servers' children, remember their birthdays, share stories about her own life. Her outfit might have been modest, but her soul was pure Chanel.

Then there was the business executive who hosted weekly meetings at our restaurant. He knew every staff member's name, from the dishwasher to the host. During the holiday season, he'd bring personalized cards for everyone. His power came not from demanding respect, but from giving it so freely that it multiplied.

These customers taught me something profound about being fancy: it's not about proving you belong in beautiful spaces — it's about creating beauty wherever you are. It's about understanding that every interaction is an opportunity to add a little sparkle to someone's day, to transform the ordinary into something special.

When I train new staff now, I tell them to watch for these truly elegant customers — the ones who make others feel valued. "That," I tell them, "is what real fancy looks like." Because true fanciness isn't something you wear — it's something you do. It's not something you demand — it's something you create.

The greatest lesson I've learned from all these years in restaurants is that being fancy is actually a form of generosity. It's about creating moments of beauty not just for yourself, but for everyone around you. When you understand this, every interaction becomes an opportunity to sprinkle a little stardust into the world.

I think about the difference between the customers who demand the best table and those who make any table the best one in the house. Between those who wear their wealth like armor and those who wear their kindness like a crown. Between those who see service as servitude and those who understand that we're all just humans trying to make life a little more beautiful for each other.

These days, when I host my own dinner parties or create events for others, I carry these lessons with me. Yes, I'll use the good china, arrange the flowers just so, fuss over every detail of the table setting. But I know now that the real magic isn't in the perfectly polished silver or the properly placed forks — it's in making everyone feel like they belong in that beautiful space we've created together.

Being fancy, truly fancy, means maintaining your sparkle even when things go wrong. It means understanding that how you treat the person refilling your water glass says you care. It means recognizing that true elegance isn't about being better than others — it's about making others feel better.

So, don't be an asshole. But more than that — be a creator of beauty. Be someone who makes others feel special. Be the kind of person who brings out the best in everyone around you. That's what it's all about — not just setting a beautiful table, but making sure everyone feels welcome at it. In the end, the most elegant thing you can do is make the world a little more beautiful, not just with your appearance or your possessions, but with your presence, your kindness, your grace.

Your authentic self: That's the kind of fancy that never goes out of style.

Finding Perfect in the Imperfect

It's one of those questions that, as a chef, I get asked constantly: "How do you cook the perfect boiled egg?" And of course, "Is there an easy-to-peel method?" For years, I was convinced there was no real science to this seemingly simple task. I would have success one day, and then repeat all the variables in the exact same way to no avail. The yolks would end up green and dry one time and too soft and runny the next. They would be easy to peel at times, and then impossible at others. Like so many things in life, what seemed simple on the surface held hidden complexities.

This quest for the perfect egg became something of an obsession. I tried different methods I'd read about or observed on cooking shows. I experimented with adding distilled vinegar to cold water, with immediately shocking them in ice water versus letting them cool naturally. I varied cooking times, started with cold eggs, tried room temperature eggs. Once, I even tried rolling the eggs in my hands to warm them before immersing them — the kind of slightly desperate measure that comes from wanting too much to get something right.

It just seemed to me that if I got it right once, surely this was the magic formula, the perfect sequence of steps and physics that would work every time. Right? Wrong! Here I was again with shells that stuck and putrid-colored yolks. I was thinking it's all a farce. These TV chefs and cookbooks were all lying to me. Maybe it was just all a plan to ruin me as a chef.

Then one weekend my friend Peter visited Atlanta from New York. He grew up helping his Chinese parents run their restaurant, Gum Joy, in Chelsea on 6th Avenue. His relationship with cooking was different from mine — less about striving for perfection and more about understanding the wisdom passed down through generations. Where I saw problems to solve, he saw traditions to honor.

That weekend, I was running my (self-proclaimed "famous") smoked trout salad special at the restaurant where I was executive chef. It was a dish that embodied my approach to cooking — frisée greens tossed with matchstick sour apples, candied pistachios, and delicately flaked wood-smoked trout in a Champagne vinaigrette, finished with a quenelle of dilled crème mousse and topped with slices of what I hoped would be perfectly cooked eggs. Like so many of my creations, it balanced on the edge between fancy and fussy, between celebration and showing off.

Peter watched me plate this dish, noticed my frustration with the eggs that weren't quite perfect, and said something that changed everything: "There's just one thing." My heart sank — I knew that tone. It was the one that all chefs hate to hear, the one that signals all your striving for perfection has somehow still fallen short.

But what Peter offered wasn't criticism — it was liberation. "I'll show you the seven-minute egg method," he said, with the quiet confidence of someone who knows that some of life's most profound truths are also the simplest. The very next day, I allowed him into the kitchen during the prep shift, something I rarely did. He showed me the method he'd learned from his parents in their restaurant kitchen, a technique passed down not through fancy culinary schools but through the practical wisdom of family tradition.

"Eureka!" I exclaimed when I saw the results. This was finally it. I tested it again and again, and wow, this truly was the miracle I had been searching for. I threw out all the eggs I had made for the salad special that night and recooked them with this ingenious method. They were perfection! I even used the phrase "seven-minute farm egg" in the description the servers were to use with guests. A new day had dawned for this chef, and thanks to Peter, I was not to be ruined by the hardboiled egg, or the soft-boiled egg, for that matter.

What Peter taught me wasn't just a technique — it was a philosophy. The secret wasn't in striving for some platonic ideal of perfection, but in understanding and respecting the nature of what you're working with. The humble egg, it turns out, had its own wisdom to share.

The method was deceptively simple: you poke a tiny hole in the shell before boiling. This allows the natural sulfur found in eggs to escape during cooking — it's the sulfur that causes that dreaded green ring around the yolk, that sign of trying too hard, of forcing things. How many times in my life had I done exactly that? Pushed too hard, held on too tight, tried to force perfection instead of letting things be what they needed to be?

This perfectly cooked egg became a metaphor for everything I'd been learning about being fancy, about being myself. Sometimes the most sophisticated solution isn't about adding more complexity — it's about understanding what's already there and giving it space to be its best self. Just as that pinhole allows the egg to release what needs releasing, sometimes we need to let go of our rigid ideas of perfection to achieve something truly beautiful.

The Seven-Minute Farm Egg

What's truly amazing about this method isn't just the consistent results — it's the bright yellowish-orange color of the yolks, their natural beauty unveiled rather than forced. The timing intervals make this the perfect method whether you're making soft eggs for ramen, slightly firmer ones for salads, or fully set ones for deviling. Like so many things in life, it's about understanding that different situations call for different approaches, but the fundamental respect for what you're working with never changes.

Ingredients:

1 to 12 large eggs (farm fresh preferred but standard eggs work well)
Approximately 3 qts. cold tap water
2 trays or 1 qt. ice

Directions:

Start pot on stove with about 4½ inches of water (use a pot that allows eggs to sit in one layer)

Bring water to boil. Don't add eggs yet

While water heats, use a clean safety pin or thumbtack to poke pinhole in smaller end of each egg

Once water reaches rapid boil, turn heat to light simmer

Add eggs one at a time, quickly and carefully to avoid breaking shells

Note: Some egg white may leak through pinholes — this is normal

Don't boil more than 12 eggs at once due to timing

Start timer when last egg is added

For medium-boiled eggs, cook exactly 7 minutes

Jumbo eggs: add 30 seconds

Small eggs: subtract 30 seconds

While eggs cook, prepare ice bath with ice and cold water

When timer stops, immediately remove eggs with slotted spoon and add to ice bath

Cool in ice bath for 5 minutes

Peel eggs under the water for easiest shell removal

The real revelation wasn't just about cooking eggs — it was about understanding that perfection often comes not from imposing our will, but from working in harmony with the nature of things. Just as I learned to respect the egg's need to release its sulfur, I learned to respect my own nature, to stop fighting against being "too fancy" or "too much" and instead find ways to let my authentic self shine through.

Like those eggs I struggled with for so long, I spent years trying to control things that just needed to be understood. I tried to hide my love of beauty, tried to tone down my fancy tendencies, tried to fit into spaces that weren't designed for someone like me. I was creating my own green rings of shame, my own stuck shells of self-doubt.

But just as Peter's simple wisdom transformed my relationship with eggs, the women and men who saw and accepted me — Karen with her ballet slippers, Miss Lilian with her beautiful home, Alice in her kitchen sanctuary — helped me understand that perfection isn't about forcing yourself to be something you're not. It's about creating the right conditions for your true self to emerge.

Now when I teach this egg technique to others, I tell them to listen for the moment when the water first begins to simmer, to watch for the exact shade of yellow in the yolk, to feel the weight of the egg in their hand before cracking it. I teach them that cooking, like living, is about paying attention to the small details while never losing sight of the larger purpose. It's about understanding that every egg, like every person, has its own timing, its own way of becoming what it's meant to be.

The perfect egg, it turns out, isn't perfect because it never fails — it's perfect because it teaches us to embrace the process, to understand that each attempt brings us closer to understanding, that each "failure" is just another lesson in patience and persistence.

Some days the shells still stick, some days the timing is off, but now I understand that's part of the journey too.

In the end, this is what being fancy really means. It's not about achieving some impossible standard of perfection. It's about creating beauty through understanding, about letting your true nature shine through, about finding the courage to be exactly who you are — whether that's a flower-picking boy, a quiche-making teen, a ballet-dancing dreamer, or a chef who finally learned to cook the perfect egg.

Because sometimes the most profound truths come wrapped in the simplest packages. Sometimes the most important lessons about being yourself come from learning to respect the humble egg. And sometimes the path to perfection isn't about changing who you are — it's about creating the right conditions for your authentic self to emerge, beautiful and whole, just as you were always meant to be.

Like that sulfur releasing through the pinhole, letting go of our need to be perfect actually allows us to become our best selves. And in the end, isn't that what we're all really cooking up — not just perfect eggs or beautiful meals or fancy parties, but lives that feel true to who we are?

So here's to the good eggs in our lives — the people who taught us to be ourselves, the lessons that showed us the way, and the courage to keep trying until we get it right. Here's to being fancy, being true, and being perfectly imperfect, just as we are.

Epilogue: On Being a Fancyboy

I'm sitting in my Atlanta condo as I write this, surrounded by what some might call too many beautiful things. There's a vase of "borrowed" magnolia blooms on my great-aunt's side table, a collection of vintage cordials catching the afternoon light, and more sets of china than any reasonable person might need. The table is set for a dinner party tonight — mixed patterns, layers of linens, perhaps a few too many candles. In other words, it's perfect.

Years ago, I would have worried about being "too much." Now I understand that too much is exactly enough when you're being true to yourself. That little boy who once hid flowers behind his back has grown into someone who makes beauty unapologetically, who understands that being fancy isn't frivolous — it's revolutionary.

Every quiche I bake, every table I set, every flower I arrange is an act of defiance against a world that once tried to shame me for loving beautiful things. But more than that, it's an act of love — for that scared boy in the loft who worried his casseroles might give him away, for the ballet dancer who lost his teacher too soon, for everyone who's ever been told they're too much, too fancy, too different.

I think often about the people who helped me become who I am: Karen, who gave me permission to dance; Miss Lilian, who showed me how to make a home truly your own; Alice, who made her kitchen a sanctuary. I think about my father, teaching me wildflower names on mountain trails, and my mother, letting me arrange her garden flowers in Mason jars. I think about Peter, who taught me that sometimes perfection comes not from trying harder, but from understanding deeper.

These days, when someone calls my style "old lady chic," I take it as the highest compliment. Because those old ladies — my grandmothers, my aunts, the women who filled their homes with beauty and their tables with love — they knew something important. They knew that making life fancy isn't about showing off or proving anything. It's about creating moments of grace in an often-graceless world. It's about turning ordinary days into celebrations, about making people feel special, about adding a bit of sparkle to even the darkest times.

So here's my invitation to you: be too much. Set that elaborate table. Pick those flowers (carefully, of course). Make that complicated recipe. Put out the good china for no reason at all. Fill your home with things that make your heart sing, even if others don't understand. Create beauty wherever you go, not because you need to prove anything, but because making things beautiful is who you are.

Because here's what I finally understand: Being fancy isn't about perfection — it's about love. Love for beauty, love for tradition, love for the simple act of making something special. It's about creating spaces where everyone feels welcome, where being different is celebrated, where there's always room for one more at the table.

And if anyone ever tells you you're too much, too fancy, too anything — just smile and add another flower to your arrangement. Because sometimes being too much is exactly what the world needs. Sometimes the most radical thing you can do is simply be yourself, in all your fancy glory.

Now, if you'll excuse me, I have a dinner party to host, and these flowers aren't going to arrange themselves.

About the Author

Walker Brown, a seasoned chef and private entertainer, grew up in a small university town on the Cumberland Plateau in Middle Tennessee. Raised in an off-the-grid, hippy-style home, he developed a passion for cooking in his family's kitchen and restaurant, using produce from his mother's expansive garden. His culinary journey led him to play a key role in shaping Atlanta Georgia's restaurant scene. Now, he brings his love of all things "fancy" to his private clients and friends.

About the Type and Paper

Designed by Malou Verlomme of the Monotype Studio, Macklin is an elegant, high-contrast typeface. It has been designed purposely for more emotional appeal.

The concept for Macklin began with research on historical material from Britain and Europe dating to the beginning of the 19th century, specifically the work of Vincent Figgins. Verlomme pays respect to Figgins's work with Macklin, but pushes the family to a more contemporary place.

This book is printed on natural Rolland Enviro Book stock. The paper is 100 percent post-consumer sustainable fiber content and is FSC-certified.

Fancyboy was designed by Eleanor Safe and Joseph Floresca.

Unbound Edition Press champions honest, original voices. Committed to the power of writers who explore and illuminate the contemporary human condition, we publish collections of poetry, short fiction, and essays. Our publisher and editorial team aim to identify, develop, and defend authors who create thoughtfully challenging work which may not find a home with mainstream publishers. We are guided by a mission to respect and elevate emerging, under-appreciated, and marginalized authors, with a strong commitment to advancing LGBTQ+ and BIPOC voices. We are honored to make meaningful contributions to the literary arts by publishing their work.

unboundedition.com